THE 50 STATES

FACT BOOK FOR KIDS

ISBN 979-8-9891101-8-6
(paperback)

Published in the United States by Big Heart Books.

BIG HEART
books

TABLE OF CONTENTS

INTRODUCTION

With 50 different states covering more than 3 million square miles, learning about the United States of America can be a daunting task, which is why we wanted to write this book: to make learning about all the fifty states fun!

That's why we've compiled 1000+ of the most fun and fascinating facts about the states and organized them into easy-to-use, kid-friendly lists you can use to unlock your knowledge about the United States.

For instance, you'll find awesome facts about each state, like:

- State capitals
- Cool state symbols like the nickname, bird, animal, and gemstone
- Unique natural features you'll find there
- Important events that happened there
- Famous places you can visit
- Well-known people who lived there
- And tons of other fun facts you'll love learning!

Whether you're learning for school, planning a road trip, or just curious about our country, this guide makes it super easy and exciting to learn about the United States.

Now, get ready to explore the 50 states like never before!

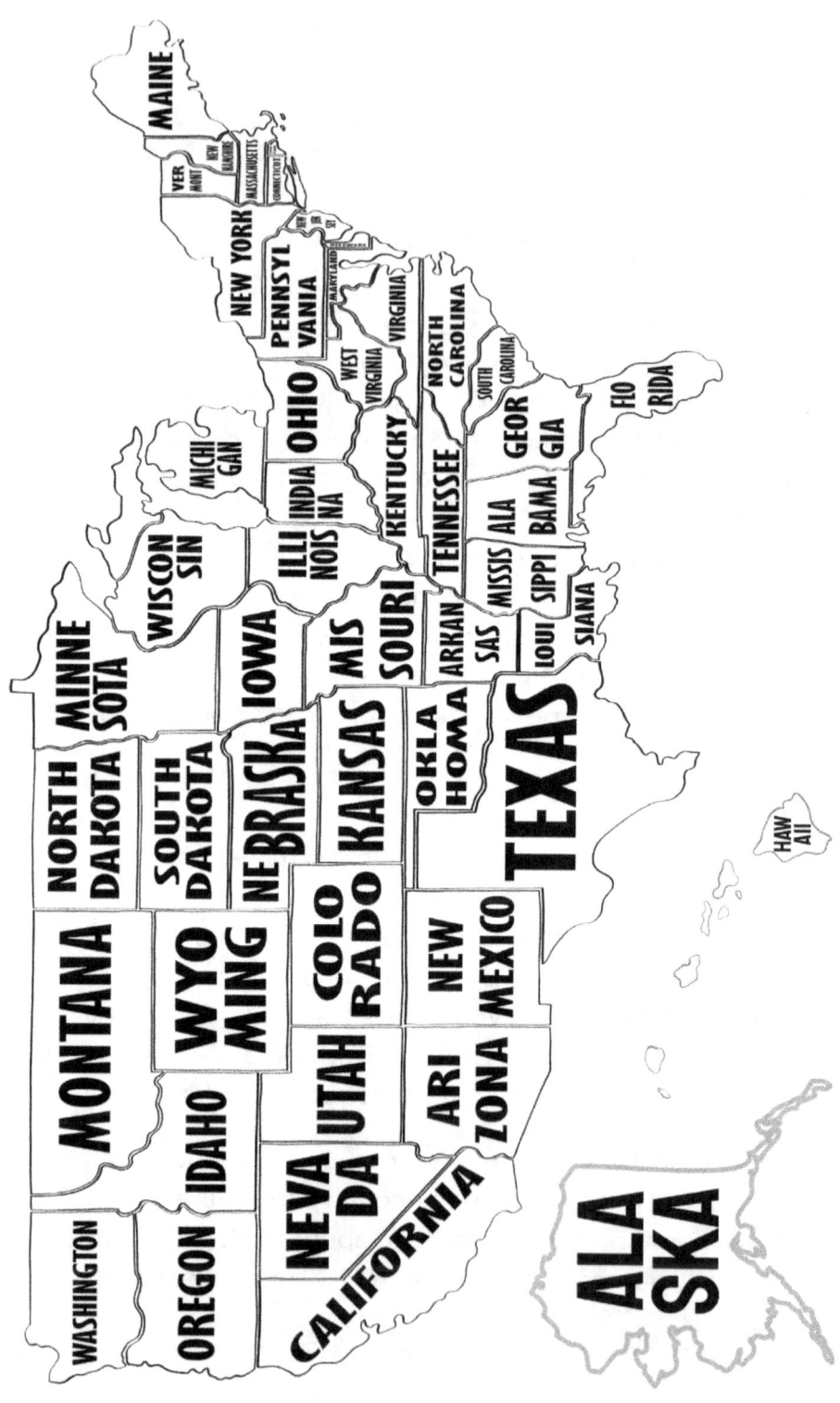

TURN LEARNING INTO AN INTERACTIVE ADVENTURE WITH THESE BEST-SELLING COMPANION BOOKS:

LEARNING THE 50 STATES HAS NEVER BEEN THIS FUN & EASY!

GET YOURS NOW!

Alabama

- **State capital:** Montgomery
- **State nickname:** The Heart of Dixie
- **State land mammal:** Black bear
- **State bird:** Yellowhammer
- **State tree:** Longleaf pine
- **State flower:** Camellia
- **State rock or gemstone:** Star blue quartz
- **State fossil:** Basilosaurus cetoides

UNIQUE NATURAL FEATURES

- **Atlantic Ocean:** Situated on the Atlantic's Gulf of Mexico (America), Alabama has its own beaches such as Gulf Shores where you can even see dolphins!

FAMOUS PLACES

- **Moundville Archaeological Park:** Home to ancient Native American burial mounds, it was once one of the largest cities north of Mexico. That's why National Geographic called it "The Big Apple of the 14th Century."
- **The USS Alabama Battleship:** Located in Mobile, kids can explore a real battleship from World War II!

• **The Civil Rights Institute:** This museum in Birmingham teaches visitors about the civil rights movement through interactive exhibits.

• **U.S. Space & Rocket Center:** Located in Huntsville, it's one of the best places to learn about space and rockets. Visitors can see real rockets and learn about space exploration!

EVENTS FROM HISTORY

• **Montgomery Bus Boycott:** Civil rights leader Rosa Parks refused to give up her bus seat on December 1, 1955 in Montgomery, sparking a mass protest.

• **Civil Rights March:** On March 25, 1965, Martin Luther King, Jr., led thousands of protestors on a 54-mile trek from through Alabama from Selma to Montgomery to try to get African Americans the right to vote.

FAMOUS PEOPLE

• **Rosa Parks:** Civil Rights icon (see above) was born in Tuskegee on February 4, 1913.

• **Helen Keller:** Born in Tuscumbia, she was both blind and deaf but learned to read and write, eventually graduating from college.

• **Harper Lee:** Born in Monroeville, Lee was the author of *To Kill a Mockingbird*, an important book about equality and justice.

OTHER FUN FACTS

• **Cotton Production**: Sometimes called "The Cotton State," Alabama once grew 23 percent of all the cotton in the U.S., though Texas now grows more.

• **Unique Food:** Alabama is famous for its delicious barbecue and fried catfish!

Alaska

- **State capital:** Juneau
- **State nickname:** Last Frontier
- **State land mammal:** Moose
- **State bird:** Willow ptarmigan
- **State tree:** Sitka spruce
- **State flower:** Forget-me-not
- **State mineral:** Gold
- **State fossil:** Woolly mammoth

UNIQUE NATURAL FEATURES

- **Coastline:** Located on the Pacific Ocean, Alaska has more coastline (more than 6,600 miles!) than all other states combined!
- **Northern Lights:** One of the world's best places to see the Northern Lights (the Aurora Borealis), when solar wind particles collide with Earth's atmosphere.

FAMOUS PLACES

- **Denali:** Formerly called Mount McKinley, it's the tallest mountain in North America, standing at 20,310 feet tall.
- **Glacier Bay National Park:** This national park features stunning glaciers and beautiful fjords.

EVENTS FROM HISTORY

• **Purchase from Russia:** Alaska was purchased from Russia in 1867 for just two cents an acre!

• **Gold Rush:** Thousands of people travelled through Alaska during the Klondike Gold Rush in the late 1890s.

• **The Alaska Statehood Act:** Signed in 1959, Alaska became the 49th state of the United States.

FAMOUS PEOPLE

• **Jack London:** The author of *The Call of the Wild* spent time in Alaska during the Klondike Gold Rush, which helped inspire the adventures in his classic book.

• **Sarah Palin:** Alaska's first female governor, she ran for United States vice president in 2008 alongside Republican presidential nominee John McCain.

OTHER FUN FACTS

• **Largest State:** Alaska is the largest state in the U.S., covering more land than Texas, California, and Montana combined!

• **Midnight Sun:** In summer, some parts of Alaska experience almost 24 hours of sunlight, while in winter, there are long periods of darkness!

• **Indigenous People:** Home to many Indigenous peoples including the Iñupiat, Yup'ik and Athabaskan.

• **Polar Bears:** Alaska is the only place in the U.S. where you can see polar bears in the wild!

• **Iditarod Trail Sled Dog Race:** An exciting annual race where teams of sled dogs race across Alaska's snowy landscape.

Arizona

- **State capital:** Phoenix
- **State nickname:** Grand Canyon State
- **State animal:** Ringtail
- **State bird:** Cactus wren
- **State tree:** Blue palo verde
- **State flower:** Saguaro cactus blossom
- **State rock or gemstone:** Turquoise
- **State fossil:** Petrified wood

UNIQUE NATURAL FEATURES

- **Deserts:** This is the only state where you'll find parts of all the "Big Four" North American deserts: the Great Basin, Mojave, Sonoran, and Chihuahuan. (The Chihuahuan is the continent's largest hot desert, and the Great Basin is its largest cold desert.)

FAMOUS PLACES

- **Grand Canyon:** One of the Seven Natural Wonders of the World, and the only one found in the United States! The national park protecting it was established in 1919 by President Woodrow Wilson.

• **Barringer Crater:** This meteorite crater is one of the best-preserved meteorite impact sites in the world.
• **Monument Valley:** Famous for its towering sandstone buttes, it is located within the Navajo Nation and is sacred to its people.
• **Petrified Forest National Park:** Located near Arizona's border with New Mexico in the Painted Desert, it's famous for Triassic-era fossils.
• **Historic Route 66:** This highway is famous for its nostalgic roadside attractions and runs through Arizona.

EVENTS FROM HISTORY
• **The Gunfight at O.K. Corral:** This famous 1881 gunfight took place between Wyatt Earp and Doc Holliday in Tombstone, Arizona.

FAMOUS PEOPLE
• **Geronimo:** An Apache leader who resisted efforts to remove his people from their land in the 1800s.
• **Cesar Chavez:** Born in Yuma, he was a civil rights activist who advocated for farmworker rights.
• **Steven Spielberg:** The famous movie director (*E.T.*, *Jurassic Park*, and *Indiana Jones*) grew up in Phoenix, where he made his first home movies as a kid!

OTHER FUN FACTS
• **Saguaro Cactus:** The iconic Saguaro cactus, which can grow to be over 40 feet tall and live for over 150 years, is native to the Sonoran Desert.
• **Native Americans:** Arizona is home to 22 Native American tribes, including the Navajo Nation, which has a rich cultural heritage and history.

Arkansas

- **State capital:** Little Rock
- **State nickname:** Natural State
- **State animal:** White-tailed deer
- **State bird:** Northern mockingbird
- **State tree:** Pine tree
- **State flower:** Apple blossom
- **State gemstone:** Diamond
- **State dinosaur:** Arkansaurus

UNIQUE NATURAL FEATURES
- **Lake Ouachita:** One of the nation's cleanest lakes, it's home to rare freshwater jellyfish that don't sting!

FAMOUS PLACES
- **Crater of Diamonds State Park:** Arkansas is the only place in the U.S. where diamonds are found in their natural state, and at this park, you can dig for real diamonds and keep what you find!
- **Hot Springs National Park:** This national park is famous for its ancient thermal springs.

EVENTS FROM HISTORY

• **Little Rock Nine:** In 1957, the Little Rock Nine were a group of African American students who helped integrate their school in Little Rock so that all kids, no matter their race, could go to school together.

FAMOUS PEOPLE

• **Hattie Caraway:** In 1931, she took on her husband's role as U.S. Senator when he died. In 1932, she was the first woman elected to the United States Senate.

• **Douglas MacArthur:** Born in Little Rock, he commanded the U.S. army in the Southwest Pacific during World War II and was a war hero.

• **Bill Clinton:** The 42nd U.S. president was born in Hope and also served as governor of the state.

• **Sam Walton:** The cofounder of Walmart opened the first store of the chain in Rogers in 1962.

OTHER FUN FACTS

• **Name Origin:** The state's name comes from a word used by French explorers to refer to the Quapaw Native American tribe, meaning "people of the south wind."

• **State Dinosaur:** Arkansas has a state dinosaur, the Arkansaurus, remains of which was discovered in the state in 1972. It was a two-legged, carnivorous dinosaur that lived during the Cretaceous period.

• **Natural State:** The state's official nickname, "The Natural State," was inspired by tourism and refers to the state's natural beauty including its various mountains, rivers, and hot springs.

California

- **State capital:** Sacramento
- **State nickname:** Golden State
- **State animal:** California grizzly bear
- **State bird:** California quail
- **State tree:** Coast redwood, giant Sequoia
- **State flower:** California Poppy
- **State rock or gemstone:** Gold
- **State fossil:** Sabre-toothed cat

UNIQUE NATURAL FEATURES
- **Tallest Trees:** Home to the tallest trees in the world, the coastal redwoods here can grow over 350 feet tall!

FAMOUS PLACES
- **Golden Gate Bridge:** An iconic suspension bridge in San Francisco, known for its stunning views and bright orange color.
- **Hollywood:** A part of Los Angeles with many movie studios and where many celebrities live. It's also where you'll find the Hollywood Walk of fame and the famous Hollywood sign that overlooks the city.

• **Disneyland:** Located in Anaheim, Disneyland was the first theme park opened by the Walt Disney Company in 1955 and is known as "The Happiest Place on Earth."

• **Yosemite National Park:** Known for its stunning granite cliffs, waterfalls, and giant sequoias, famous sites here include El Capitan, Yosemite Falls, and the Mariposa Grove of Giant Sequoias.

• **Death Valley National Park:** The hottest, driest, and lowest national park, it is known for its extreme temperatures and unique geological features.

• **Silicon Valley:** This region is home to many famous tech companies, including Apple, Google, and Facebook.

EVENTS FROM HISTORY

• **Gold Rush:** The California Gold Rush in the mid-1800s attracted thousands of people seeking fortune and led to a rapid population growth.

FAMOUS PEOPLE

• **John Wayne:** The Western movie star spent much of his childhood in Glendale and first acquired his nickname "Duke" while living in California.

• **Steve Jobs:** Born in San Francisco, the cofounder of Apple grew up in what later became known as Silicon Valley, where he first started his company.

OTHER FUN FACTS

• **Population:** California is the state with the highest population in the country.

• **National Parks:** California has more National Parks than any other U.S. state!

Colorado

- **State capital:** Denver
- **State nickname:** Centennial State
- **State animal:** Rocky Mountain bighorn sheep
- **State bird:** Lark bunting
- **State tree:** Colorado blue spruce
- **State flower:** Colorado blue columbine
- **State rock or gemstone:** Aquamarine
- **State fossil:** Stegosaurus

UNIQUE NATURAL FEATURES

- **Mountains:** About half of Colorado is covered by mountains, most of which is the Rocky Mountains. In fact, Colorado has 53 "fourteeners," mountains over 14,000 feet tall, including the famous Plke's Peak.
- **The Continental Divide:** This line runs north to south through Colorado's Rocky Mountains and separates the continent's river systems and the direction they flow.
- **Grand Mesa:** Located in western Colorado, this is the world's largest flat-topped mountain and is said to look like a giant table!

FAMOUS PLACES

- **Rocky Mountain National Park:** It is one of the highest national parks in the country, with sixty mountain peaks more than 12,000 feet high.
- **Mesa Verde National Park:** Where Ancestral Pueblo people built homes into cliffs almost a thousand years ago, the park features over 4,700 archaeological sites, including 600 of these cliff dwellings.
- **Mile High City:** Denver is known as the Mile High City because it sits exactly one mile above sea level.

EVENTS FROM HISTORY

- **Beautiful Inspiration:** The poem "America the Beautiful" was written in 1893 by Katherine Lee Bates. It was, in part, inspired by a visit to Pike's Peak with its "purple mountain majesties."

FAMOUS PEOPLE

- **Madeleine Albright:** Born in Denver, she became the first female U.S. Secretary of State, helping shape American foreign policy in the 1990s.
- **Scott Carpenter:** A native of Boulder, he was one of the original seven NASA astronauts and helped explore space during the Mercury missions.

OTHER FUN FACTS

- **Name Origin:** Colorado is named after the Spanish word for "colored red," because of its reddish soil.
- **Centennial State:** Colorado got its nickname because it became the 38th U.S. state in 1876, exactly 100 years after the Declaration of Independence was signed.

Connecticut

- **State capital:** Hartford
- **State nickname:** The Constitution State
- **State animal:** Sperm whale
- **State bird:** American robin
- **State tree:** White oak
- **State flower:** Mountain laurel
- **State rock or gemstone:** Garnet
- **State fossil:** Dinosaur tracks

UNIQUE NATURAL FEATURES

- **Connecticut River:** Divides the state roughly in half.
- **Fall Leaves:** The state is famous for colorful fall leaves, inspiring visitors to go "leaf peeping" in autumn.

FAMOUS PLACES

- **Oldest Public Library:** The Scoville Memorial Library, founded in 1771, is the U.S.'s oldest public library.
- **Yale University:** Located in New Haven, Yale is one of the nation's oldest and most prestigious universities.

EVENTS FROM HISTORY

- **Revolutionary War:** When war broke out in 1775, Connecticut was one of the first colonies to join the fight.

• **Speed Limits:** Connecticut was the first state to establish speed limits for cars in 1901.

FAMOUS PEOPLE

• **Noah Webster:** He wrote the first American dictionary in this state.
• **Nathan Hale:** A famous spy for General George Washington during the Revolutionary War. When he was caught and sentenced to death by the British, he famously said, "I only regret that I have but one life to lose for my country."
• **Mark Twain:** The famous author (whose real name was Samuel Clemens) known for books like *Tom Sawyer* and *Huckleberry Finn*, lived in Hartford, where you can still visit his house and a museum dedicated to him.
• **Harriet Beecher Stowe:** Born in Connecticut, she was the author of *Uncle Tom's Cabin*, which helped raised awareness of how bad slavery was.

OTHER FUN FACTS

• **Nutmeg State:** Connecticut is often referred to as the "Nutmeg State" because its early inhabitants were said to be so clever and resourceful that they could get people to buy (worthless!) wooden nutmegs!
• **Provisions State:** Another nickname for Connecticut is the "Provisions State" because during the Revolutionary War, it provided a significant amount of food and cannons for the Continental forces.
• **Small Size:** Connecticut is the third smallest state in the country, after Rhode Island and Delaware.

Delaware

- **State capital:** Dover
- **State nickname:** The First State
- **State animal:** Grey fox
- **State bird:** Delaware Blue hen
- **State tree:** American holly
- **State flower:** Peach blossom
- **State rock or gemstone:** Sillimanite
- **State fossil:** Belemnite

UNIQUE NATURAL FEATURES

- **Waterfront:** Situated on the Atlantic Ocean on a peninsula called the Delmarva, the state also features the Delaware River and Delaware Bay.
- **The Great Cypress Swamp:** It is the northernmost cypress swamp in the United States with cypress trees that are hundreds of years old.

FAMOUS PLACES

- **First State Heritage Park:** In Dover, this historic (and national!) park celebrates 18th-century life and preserves Colonial landmarks like the Old State House.
- **Bombay Hook National Wildlife Refuge:** A tidal salt marsh, it is where you can find many migrating birds.

- **Dover International Speedway:** This NASCAR raceway is nicknamed the Monster Mile, with a 46-foot statue of a monster holding a full-size car near the track.

EVENTS FROM HISTORY

- **State Origins:** Delaware was originally part of the Pennsylvania colony, but broke away to announce its independence from Great Britain weeks before the enactment of the Declaration of Independence in 1776.
- **The Constitution:** On December 7, 1787, it was the first of the 13 original colonies to ratify the federal Constitution following the Revolutionary War.

FAMOUS PEOPLE

- **Henry Heimlich:** Born in Delaware, he developed the "Heimlich maneuver" in 1976 to save choking victims.
- **Joe Biden:** The 46th President of the United States, he moved to Delaware as a kid and served as a Delaware Senator from 1973 until 2009, when he became U.S. Vice President under Barak Obama.

OTHER FUN FACTS

- **State Name Origins:** Delaware was named after the Delaware River, which was named after Lord De La Warr, who oversaw the Virginia colony.
- **First State:** Delaware earned this nickname because it was the first state to ratify the U.S. Constitution in 1787.
- **Small Size:** Delaware is the second-smallest state in the country. Only Rhode Island is smaller!

Florida

- **State capital:** Tallahassee
- **State nickname:** The Sunshine State
- **State animal:** Florida panther
- **State bird:** Northern mockingbird
- **State tree:** Sabal palm
- **State flower:** Orange blossom
- **State rock or gemstone:** Moonstone
- **State fossil:** Agatized Coral

UNIQUE NATURAL FEATURES
- **Peninsula:** Florida is a peninsula, which means it is almost completely surrounded by water.
- **Waterfront:** Situated with the Atlantic Ocean to its east and the Gulf of Mexico (America) to its west, Florida is surrounded by water with many wetlands and swamps.

FAMOUS PLACES
- **Everglades National Park:** The largest tropical wilderness in the U.S., it's the only place in the world where alligators and crocodiles coexist together!

• **Cape Canaveral:** Home to NASA's Kennedy Space Center, it has been the launch site for many historic space missions, including the Apollo moon missions.
• **Florida Keys:** This coral cay archipelago made up of 1,700 tiny islands, which are interconnected by a causeway and 42 various bridges.
• **Orlando:** Known as the "Theme Park Capital of the World," where you'll find multiple theme parks, including Walt Disney World, Universal Studios Florida, and SeaWorld Orlando.

EVENTS FROM HISTORY

• **Fountain of Youth:** Spanish explorer Ponce de Leon arrived in St. Augustine in 1513 where he found a fountain that he called the Fountain of Youth.
• **Spain Exchange:** Florida was treated as a colony of both Spain and Great Britain until Spain gave Florida to the U.S. in 1821 in exchange for Spanish rule in Texas.

FAMOUS PEOPLE

• **Ariana Grande:** Born in Boca Raton, the famous singer and actress has starred in hits like *Wicked*.
• **Zora Neale Hurston:** The author of the literary classic *Their Eyes Were Watching God* was born in Eatonville.

OTHER FUN FACTS

• **State Name Origins:** Ponce de Leon named the area La Florida, which means "the land of flowers."
• **Orange Origins:** Many believe Ponce de Leon was the first to plant orange seeds in Florida! Today, the state is a leading orange producer.

Georgia

- **State capital:** Atlanta
- **State nickname:** The Peach State
- **State animal:** White-tailed deer
- **State bird:** Brown thrasher
- **State tree:** Live oak
- **State flower:** Cherokee rose
- **State rock or gemstone:** Quartz
- **State fossil:** Megalodon shark tooth

UNIQUE NATURAL FEATURES

- **Okefenokee Swamp:** At 700 square miles in size, it's the largest blackwater swamp in North America.
- **Georgia Islands:** Georgia has 15 barrier islands off its coast in the Atlantic; you can vacation at four of them.
- **Lookout Mountain:** Situated near the state's border with Tennessee and Alabama, you can see seven states from the top of this 2,393-foot-tall mountain!

FAMOUS PLACES

- **The Georgia Aquarium:** Located in Atlanta, it is one of the largest aquariums in the world, with marine life including dolphins and whale sharks!

• **Centennial Park:** This 22-acre park was built for the 1996 Summer Olympic Games in the heart of Atlanta.
• **The Varsity:** Stretching over two city blocks in Atlanta, this is the world's largest drive-in restaurant!

EVENTS FROM HISTORY

• **13th Colony:** In 1733, Georgia was established as the 13th of the original Thirteen Colonies.
• **Civil War Battlegrounds:** Georgia is home to prominent Civil War battlefields including Chickamauga, Resaca, and Kennesaw Mountain.

FAMOUS PEOPLE

• **Martin Luther King, Jr:** He was born and raised in Atlanta before becoming a pastor and pivotal Civil Rights leader.
• **Jimmy Carter:** The 39th president of the United States, Carter grew up here, originally as a peanut farmer. Visit his boyhood home, which includes a 13-foot-tall peanut sculpture!

OTHER FUN FACTS

• **State Name Origins:** The state was named after England's King George II.
• **Watermelon Capital:** Cordele is known as the "Watermelon Capital of the World" and celebrates the fruit with an annual festival every summer.
• **Peanuts Aplenty:** Georgia grows the most peanuts in the country. Plus, a popular snack here is boiled peanuts!
• **Vidalia Onions:** Known for its sweet flavor, Vidalia onions can only be grown here in Georgia.

Hawaii

- **State capital:** Honolulu
- **State nickname:** Aloha State
- **State animal:** Hawaiian monk seal
- **State bird:** Nēnē (Hawaiian goose)
- **State tree:** Kukui tree (candlenut tree)
- **State flower:** Yellow hibiscus
- **State rock or gemstone:** Black coral
- **State fossil:** None designated

UNIQUE NATURAL FEATURES

- **Chain of Islands:** Hawaii is the only U.S. state made up completely of islands—137, in fact! But people only live on 7 of them: Hawaii (called the Big Island), Maui, Molokai, Lanai, Oahu, Kauai, and Niihau.
- **Volcanoes:** Hawaii is made entirely of volcanoes that started erupting over 70 million years ago; six of them are still active volcanoes today!
- **Rainforests:** The state is home to lush rainforests, which are especially found on the windward sides of the islands.
- **Beaches:** You can find Hawaiian beaches with white, black, red and even green sand. In fact, there are only four green sand beaches in the world!

FAMOUS PLACES

• **Pearl Harbor:** A historic World War II site where the USS Arizona Memorial honors those who lost their lives during the attack on Pearl Harbor in 1941.
• **Hawai'i Volcanoes National Park:** It is home to Hawaii's most active volcano, Kilauea.
• **Haleakalā National Park:** Located on Maui, it is home to the world's largest dormant volcano.
• **North Shore:** Known as the "Seven Mile Miracle," this stretch of coastline is famous to surfers around the world.

EVENTS FROM HISTORY

• **Ancient Polynesian Culture:** Hawaii was settled by Polynesians who navigated thousands of miles in special canoes across the Pacific Ocean.
• **King Kamehameha:** In 1810, he unified the Hawaiian islands into a single kingdom and became the Kingdom of Hawaii's first ruler.
• **50th State:** Hawaii became the last U.S. state in 1959.

FAMOUS PEOPLE

• **Barack Obama:** The 44th president of the United States was born in Honolulu.

OTHER FUN FACTS

• **Bilingual:** Hawaii is the only U.S. state with two official languages: English and Hawaiian.
• **Vacation Hotspot:** Tourism is the state's leading source of income, attracting millions of tourists each year.
• **Rare Animals:** Some animals in Hawaii are found nowhere else in the world, including the Hawaiian monk seal (which is the state animal) and the nēnē (which is the state bird).

Idaho

- **State capital:** Boise
- **State nickname:** Gem State
- **State horse:** Appaloosa horse
- **State bird:** Mountain bluebird
- **State tree:** Western white pine
- **State flower:** Syringa
- **State rock or gemstone:** Star garnet
- **State fossil:** Hagerman horse

UNIQUE NATURAL FEATURES

- **Hot Springs:** With about 130 soakable hot springs, Idaho has more usable natural hot springs than any other U.S. state.
- **Rocky Mountains:** They stretch through the middle of the state and are where you'll find the state's highest point, Borah Peak.
- **Hell's Canyon:** The deepest river gorge in North America, it's even deeper than the Grand Canyon!

FAMOUS PLACES

- **Shoshone Falls:** Located on the Snake River, this stunning 212-foot-tall waterfall is sometimes called "the Niagara of the West," and is actually taller than Niagara Falls!

- **Craters of the Moon National Monument & Preserve:** This unique volcanic landscape is named because its vast oceans of lava flows and cinder cones look like the surface of the moon!
- **Silver City:** An old mining town, it looks almost exactly the same way it did more than a hundred years ago!

EVENTS FROM HISTORY

- **Native Americans & First Explorers:** Various Native American tribes have lived in Idaho for more than 13,000 years. The first non-native people to visit were explorers Mariwether Lewis and William Clark in 1805.
- **Gold Rush Beginnings:** Gold was discovered in Idaho in 1860, causing thousands of people to move here. By 1863, it became its own territory, and became the 43rd state in 1890.

FAMOUS PEOPLE

- **Sacagawea:** This Lemhi Shoshone woman was a crucial guide and interpreter for explorers Lewis and Clark.
- **Ernest Hemingway:** The famous author spent his last years in Ketchum, where he died and is now buried.

OTHER FUN FACTS

- **State Name Origins:** While some thought "Idaho" was a Native American word meaning "gem of the mountains," it actually is a made-up word!
- **Potatoes:** Idaho is famous for growing the most potatoes in the country—about 13 billion pounds each year!—and even has a potato museum.

Illinois

- **State capital:** Springfield
- **State nickname:** The Prairie State
- **State animal:** White-tailed deer
- **State bird:** Northern cardinal
- **State tree:** White oak
- **State flower:** Violet
- **State mineral:** Fluorite
- **State fossil:** Tully monster

UNIQUE NATURAL FEATURES

- **Waterways:** Illinois is bordered by Lake Michigan to the northeast, the Ohio River to the south, and the Mississippi River along the west side of the state.

FAMOUS PLACES

- **Millennium Park:** Built in 2004, the park is famous for its Cloud Gate sculpture (also known as "The Bean") and beautiful gardens.
- **Navy Pier:** Located along Lake Michigan, it is a tourist destination known for its Centennial Wheel that offers 360-degree views of the city.
- **The Willis Tower:** Formerly known as the Sears Tower, this skyscraper remains one of the tallest buildings in the

country. You can even stand on a glass ledge and look down over Chicago!

EVENTS FROM HISTORY

• **Abolishing Slavery:** Illinois was the first state to ratify the 13th Amendment to the Constitution, which abolished slavery.

• **The Great Chicago Fire:** In 1871, a huge fire tore through Chicago for three days, killing 300 people and leaving 100,000 without homes.

• **First Skyscraper:** Built in 1885, the Home Life Insurance Building was considered the world's first skyscraper, at 10 stories tall. The building was demolished in 1971, though.

FAMOUS PEOPLE

• **Abraham Lincoln:** The 16th president lived in Springfield before being elected president. In fact, Illinois is known as the "Land of Lincoln."

• **Jane Addams:** A famous activist from Chicago, she co-founded the Hull House to support immigrants and poor families—and won the Nobel Peace Prize for it!

• **Walt Disney:** The creator of Mickey Mouse was born and spent his early years in Chicago before becoming a pioneer of animator.

OTHER FUN FACTS

• **Pizza, Pizza!:** Chicago is known as the birthplace of deep-dish pizza.

• **Tully Monster:** Fossil remains of this unique sea creature were discovered in 1958 and have only been found in Illinois. It's so unique that scientists still don't agree about what kind of animal it was!

Indiana

- **State capital:** Indianapolis
- **State nickname:** Hoosier State
- **State animal:** None designated
- **State bird:** Northern cardinal
- **State tree:** Tulip tree
- **State flower:** Peony
- **State rock or gemstone:** Limestone
- **State fossil:** American mastodon

UNIQUE NATURAL FEATURES

- **Indiana Dunes National Park:** A unique area featuring sandy beaches, dunes, and diverse ecosystems along Lake Michigan, which forms the state's northern border.
- **Terrain:** With flat terrain in the north and rolling hills in the south, its land is ideal for farming and agriculture.

FAMOUS PLACES

- **Indianapolis Motor Speedway:** Home to the Indianapolis 500, the oldest major car race in the world, it's known as the "greatest spectacle in racing."

- **The Children's Museum of Indianapolis:** The largest children's museum in the world, it offers a variety of interactive exhibits and educational experiences specifically designed for kids!

EVENTS FROM HISTORY

- **Lyles Station:** Founded in the 1800s by free Black settlers, it is one of the only African American settlements from that time still around today!
- **Polio Vaccine:** In 1954, Dr. Jonas Salk tested this vaccine on children in Indiana, helping stop the disease that had made thousands of kids very sick.

FAMOUS PEOPLE

- **Tecumseh:** The Shawnee chief led resistance against U.S. encroachment on Native American land in 1800s. He was a key figure during the War of 1812.
- **Gus Grissom:** Born in Mitchell, he was the second American to fly in space. He was also one of NASA's original Mercury Seven and flew the first crewed mission of the Gemini Program.
- **Larry Bird:** Born in French Lick, he played for the Boston Celtics from 1979 to 1992 and is regarded as one of the greatest basketball players of all time.
- **Madam C.J. Walker:** While living in Indianapolis, she built a hair-care and cosmetic line for Black women and became the first self-made female millionaire in the U.S.!

OTHER FUN FACTS

- **Crossroads of America:** Indiana earned this nickname because it's located at the intersection of four major highways, making it a key transportation hub.

Iowa

- **State capital:** Des Moines
- **State nickname:** The Hawkeye State
- **State animal:** None designated
- **State bird:** Eastern goldfinch
- **State tree:** Oak
- **State flower:** Wild rose
- **State rock or gemstone:** Geode

UNIQUE NATURAL FEATURES
- **River Borders:** Iowa is bordered by the Missouri River to the west and the Mississippi River to the east.
- **Fertile Farmland:** The state is known for having some of the best soil in the world. In fact, approximately 92 percent of Iowa's land is used for farming!

FAMOUS PLACES
- **Field of Dreams:** The iconic baseball diamond from this film is located in Dyersville.
- **Iowa State Fair:** One of the largest state fairs in the U.S., it is famous for its giant butter cow sculpture!

EVENTS FROM HISTORY

- **The Underground Railroad:** Iowa played a significant role in the Underground Railroad, helping many escaped slaves find freedom.
- **Presidential Caucuses**: Each year, Iowa hosts the first major event in the U.S. presidential election process, known as the Iowa Caucus, where voters gather to help choose the next presidential candidates.

FAMOUS PEOPLE

- **Herbert Hoover:** The 31st President of the United States, he was born in West Branch and was known for helping feed Europe after World War I and responding to the Great Depression.
- **Grant Wood**: From Iowa, he was famous for paintings depicting rural American Midwest. His most famous is *American Gothic* of a farmer and his daughter in front of a farmhouse.
- **John Wayne:** Famous for starring as a cowboy in Hollywood movies, he was originally born in Winterset.

OTHER FUN FACTS

- **Corn Production:** Iowa grows the most corn of any state in the U.S.!
- **The First Tractor:** The first gas-powered tractor was invented in Charles City in 1892.
- **Nickname Origin:** Iowa earned its nickname "The Hawkeye State" in 1838, primarily through efforts to honor Chief Black Hawk of the Sauk tribe and to preserve his legacy.

Kansas

- **State capital:** Topeka
- **State nickname:** Sunflower State
- **State animal:** American bison
- **State bird:** Western meadowlark
- **State tree:** Eastern cottonwood
- **State flower:** Sunflower
- **State rock or gemstone:** Galena
- **State flying fossil:** Pteranodon

UNIQUE NATURAL FEATURES

- **Tallgrass Prairies:** Kansas is home to some of the most expansive prairie ecosystems in the United States.
- **Sand Dunes:** Western Kansas is known for sand dunes that can rise up to 60 feet tall!

FAMOUS PLACES

- **Monument Rocks (The Chalk Pyramids):** Natural limestone formations were created by ancient seas and are some of the state's most recognizable landmarks.

EVENTS FROM HISTORY

• **The Kansas-Nebraska Act of 1854:** This legislation created the territories of Kansas and Nebraska and allowed settlers to decide whether they would permit slavery in the years leading up to the Civil War.

• **Transcontinental Railroad:** In the 1860s, railroad was laid through Kansas that helped connect the East and West coasts of the United States.

• **Dust Bowl:** During the 1930s, Kansas experienced severe drought and powerful dust storms that destroyed crops and devastated family farms.

FAMOUS PEOPLE

• **Dwight D. Eisenhower:** Raised in Abilene, he became the 34th U.S. president and served as Supreme Commander of the Allied Expeditionary Force during World War II.

• **Amelia Earhart:** Born in Atchison, she became the first woman to fly solo across the Atlantic Ocean in 1932.

• **Langston Hughes:** The poet and author grew up in Lawrence and is famous for his role in the Harlem Renaissance writing about African American life.

OTHER FUN FACTS

• **Breadbasket of America:** The state has been called this because it is a major producer of wheat and sorghum, essential ingredients used to make bread.

• **The Wizard of Oz:** In this book (and later movie, starring Judy Garland), Dorothy's home is Kansas, which brought international fame to the state.

• **Wind Power:** Kansas is one of the top U.S. states for capturing and generating wind energy.

Kentucky

- **State capital:** Frankfort
- **State nickname:** The Bluegrass State
- **State horse:** Thoroughbred
- **State bird:** Northern cardinal
- **State tree:** Tulip poplar
- **State flower:** Goldenrod
- **State gemstone:** Freshwater pearl
- **State fossil:** Brachiopod

UNIQUE NATURAL FEATURES

- **Rivers:** Rivers form boundaries around much of Kentucky s: the Ohio River to the north, the Mississippi River to the west, and the Big Sandy River and Tug Fork on parts of its eastern border.

FAMOUS PLACES

- **Churchill Downs:** The location of the Kentucky Derby (a thoroughbred horse race), it is the longest-running sporting event in the U.S., first run 1875.
- **Mammoth Cave National Park:** With over 400 miles of explored caves, this is the longest known cave system in the world!

- **The Louisville Slugger Museum:** The family-owned brand has been creating its famous baseball bats since 1884 and here you can learn more and even see how they are made!
- **National Corvette Museum:** View all kinds of Chevrolet Corvettes and learn about their history.
- **The Ark Encounter:** Featuring a life-size replica of Noah's Ark, this museum offers educational experiences about biblical stories and history.
- **Cumberland Falls:** Known as the "Niagara of the South," it's the only place in the Western Hemisphere to see a moonbow, a rainbow created by the moon!

EVENTS FROM HISTORY
- **Wilderness Road:** Daniel Boone helped establish this path through the Cumberland Gap in 1775, allowing settlers to travel west through Kentucky.

FAMOUS PEOPLE
- **Daniel Boone:** A vital part of Kentucky's frontier history, he is known for founding one of the first English settlements west of the Appalachian Mountains and helping settlers to move west.
- **Abraham Lincoln:** America's 16th president, he was born in a log cabin in Hodgenville in 1809.
- **Muhammed Ali:** Considered one of the greatest boxers of all time, he was born and raised in Louisville.

OTHER FUN FACTS
- **Kentucky Fried Chicken:** The chain got its start Colonel Sanders began selling fried chicken in Corbin during the Great Depression.

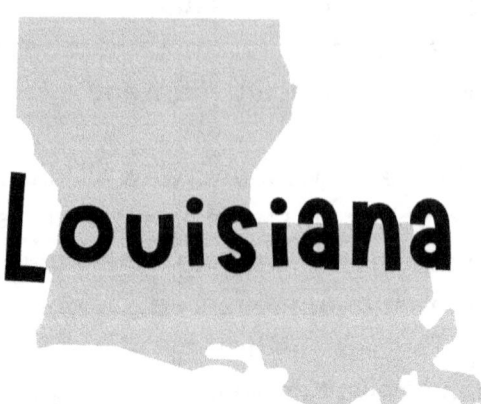

Louisiana

- **State capital:** Baton Rouge
- **State nickname:** Pelican State
- **State mammal:** Black bear
- **State bird:** Brown pelican
- **State tree:** Bald cypress
- **State flower:** Magnolia
- **State mineral:** Agate
- **State fossil:** Petrified palm wood

UNIQUE NATURAL FEATURES

- **Mississippi River Delta:** Located at the mouth of the Mississippi River, Louisiana is a key spot where the river meets the Gulf of Mexico.
- **Atchafalaya Basin:** The largest river swamp in the country, it contains almost a million acres of wetlands, bayous, and backwater lakes.

FAMOUS PLACES

- **The American Rose Center:** The nation's largest rose garden, featuring over 20,000 rose bushes!
- **The French Quarter:** New Orleans' oldest

neighborhood, it is famous for its unique architecture, food and entertainment.

EVENTS FROM HISTORY

• **Ancient Mound Site:** Known as the Watson Brake, it is one of the oldest earthwork mound complexes in North America, dating back over 5,000 years!

• **French Settlement:** During the 17th century, Louisiana began to be explored and settled by the French, resulting in a strong French influence still evident today.

• **Louisiana Purchase:** In 1803, the United States bought Louisiana from France, doubling the size of the country.

• **Hurricane Katrina:** In 2005, this massive storm resulted in flooding and damage that changed the city and inspired rebuilding efforts.

FAMOUS PEOPLE

• **Louis Armstrong:** Born in New Orleans, Louis Armstrong was a legendary jazz musician who made songs like "What a Wonderful World" famous.

• **Ruby Bridges:** In 1960, she helped end segregation by attending an otherwise all-white school in New Orleans.

OTHER FUN FACTS

• **Mardi Gras:** New Orleans famously celebrates Mardi Gras (or "Fat Tuesday") before the start of Lent with parades, music, and more.

• **Cultural Cuisine:** Louisiana is famous for Creole and Cajun food, which includes gumbo and jambalaya.

• **Jazz Music:** New Orleans is known as the birthplace of this style of music.

• **Name Origins:** French explorer Robert Cavelier de La Salle named the land to honor King Louis XIV of France.

Maine

- **State capital:** Augusta
- **State nickname:** Pine Tree State
- **State animal:** Moose
- **State bird:** Chickadee
- **State tree:** Eastern white pine
- **State flower:** White pine cone and tassel
- **State gemstone:** Tourmaline
- **State fossil:** Pertica quadrifaria

UNIQUE NATURAL FEATURES
- **Forests:** Maine has the highest percent of forest cover of any state in the U.S.: about 83% of its land is covered in forests, inspiring its nickname, the Pine Tree State.

FAMOUS PLACES
- **Appalachian Trail:** The north end of this famous hiking trail starts in Maine's Baxter State Park before winding all the way to Georgia.
- **Acadia National Park:** Home to Cadillac Mountain, where you can view the "nation's first sunrise" each day.

- **Paul Bunyan Statue:** Located in Bangor and standing 31 feet tall, it claims to be the world's largest statue of the folk-tale lumberjack.
- **Lighthouses:** Even though Michigan actually has more lighthouses, Maine has been called "The Lighthouse State" with 65 lighthouses found along its coast, inlets and various islands.

EVENTS FROM HISTORY

- **Native Americans:** The land was originally home to Native American tribes known as the Wabanaki, or "People of the Dawnland."
- **War of 1812:** British captured portions of eastern Maine, holding onto it until England surrendered and the war ended.
- **Statehood:** In 1820, Maine broke away from Massachusetts to become the 23rd sate as part of the Missouri Compromise.
- **The Aroostook War:** From 1838 to 1839, Maine almost went to war with Canada over a border dispute before resolving peacefully.

FAMOUS PEOPLE

- **E.B. White:** The author famous of *Charlotte's Web* and *Stuart Little* lived here and you can still visit his former farm and farmhouse in North Brooklin.
- **Stephen King:** The best-selling author was born and attended college in Maine, which is said to have inspired much of his writing.

OTHER FUN FACTS

- **Lobster:** Producing the most lobster in the U.S., Maine is famous for seafood dishes like lobster rolls.

Maryland

- **State capital:** Annapolis
- **State nickname:** Old Line State
- **State horse:** Thoroughbred
- **State bird:** Baltimore oriole
- **State tree:** White oak
- **State flower:** Black-eyed Susan
- **State gemstone:** Patuxent River stone agate
- **State fossil:** Ecphora gardnerae

UNIQUE NATURAL FEATURES

- **America in Miniature:** Maryland is often called this or "Little America" because it has almost every type of natural feature you can find in the United States, except for a desert!
- **Diverse Geography:** You'll find the Appalachian Mountains to the west and the Chesapeake Bay and Atlantic Ocean to the east.

FAMOUS PLACES

- **America's First Highway:** Route 40 in Cumberland was once the starting point of the National Road, America's first major highway for pioneers heading west! You can still drive it today as a Scenic Byway.

• **Antietam National Battlefield:** The Battle of Antietam in 1862 was the bloodiest single day of the Civil War, inspiring President Lincoln to issue the Emancipation Proclamation soon after.

EVENTS FROM HISTORY

• **Washington, D.C.:** Maryland and Virginia each gave up land to help create Washington, D.C., the nation's capital, in 1790.

• **Star-Spangled Banner:** The U.S. National Anthem was written when Francis Scott Key witnessed the battle at Fort McHenry during the War of 1812.

FAMOUS PEOPLE

• **Frederick Douglass:** He was born in Maryland into slavery in 1818 but later escaped to became a powerful antislavery activist.

• **Babe Ruth:** The legendary baseball Hall of Famer was born in Baltimore where a museum is dedicated to him.

• **Thurgood Marshall:** The first African American justice of the Supreme Court was born and raised in Baltimore.

OTHER FUN FACTS

• **Old Line State:** George Washington gave this nickname to the state when Maryland soldiers helped save the Continental Army during an important Revolutionary War battle.

• **Name Origin:** The name "Maryland" honors Queen Henrietta Maria, the wife of King Charles I of England.

• **Blue Crabs:** The state is famous for this unique seafood found here!

Massachusetts

- **State capital:** Boston
- **State nickname:** Bay State
- **State marine mammal:** Right whale
- **State bird:** Black-capped chickadee
- **State tree:** American elm
- **State flower:** Mayflower
- **State gemstone:** Rhodonite
- **State fossil:** Dinosaur tracks

UNIQUE NATURAL FEATURES

- **Bay State:** The state gets its nickname due to the numerous bays along its Atlantic Ocean coastline.
- **Cape Cod:** This hook-shaped peninsula sticks out into the Atlantic Ocean and is a great place to see seals.

FAMOUS PLACES

- **Boston Common:** Established in 1634, it is America's oldest public park and consists of 50 acres of land.
- **Harvard University:** The oldest institution of higher learning in the United States, it was founded in 1636.
- **Freedom Trail:** This 2.5-mile-long path through Boston leads to 16 important historical sites significant to early American history, including the Paul Revere House.

• **Fenway Park:** Opened in 1912 in Boston, it's the oldest Major League Baseball stadium and is still home to the Boston Red Sox.

EVENTS FROM HISTORY

• **Mayflower Landing:** The ship landed at Plymouth Rock on December 18, 1620 with English Pilgrims who helped start one of America's earliest colonies.
• **Thanksgiving:** In Plymouth, the Pilgrims and Wampanoag people shared a feast after the harvest in 1621, remembered today as the First Thanksgiving!
• **Boston Tea Party:** Colonists protested against British taxes by dumping tea into the Boston Harbor on December 16, 1773.
• **Paul Revere's Midnight Ride:** In April 1775, he warned locals that "The British are coming!" before the first battles of the Revolutionary War broke out.

FAMOUS PEOPLE

• **Benjamin Franklin:** One of America's Founding Fathers and a great inventor was born in Boston in 1706.
• **Johnny Appleseed (John Chapman):** Known for planting apple seeds across America's frontier, he was born in Leominster in 1774.
• **Dr. Seuss (Theodor Seuss Geisel):** Beloved author of children's books like *The Cat in the Hat* was born here.
• **Susan B. Anthony:** An important activist for women's rights was born here in 1820.

OTHER FUN FACTS

• **Basketball Birthplace:** The game was invented here in 1891 by Dr. James Naismith as a way to keep students active during the winter!

Michigan

- **State capital:** Lansing
- **State nickname:** The Wolverine State
- **State game mammal:** White-tailed deer
- **State bird:** American robin
- **State tree:** Eastern white pine
- **State flower:** Apple blossom
- **State rock or gemstone:** Petoskey stone
- **State fossil:** American mastodon

UNIQUE NATURAL FEATURES

- **Great Lakes:** Michigan borders four of the five Great Lakes: Lake Michigan, Lake Huron, Lake Erie, and Lake Superior.
- **Mitten Shape:** The state is famously shaped like a mitten, making it easy to find on a map!

FAMOUS PLACES

- **Detroit:** Known as the "Car Capital of the World," Detroit is home to Ford, General Motors, and Chrysler.
- **Mackinac Island:** A unique island known for its ban on motor vehicles since 1898. Visitors instead travel by horse-drawn carriage, bike, or on foot.

EVENTS FROM HISTORY

- **Battle of Lake Erie:** This battle took place during the War of 1812, when American naval forces kept control of the Great Lakes by defeating the British.
- **Assembly Line:** Henry Ford revolutionized manufacturing when he introduced this concept in 1913 in his Highland Park factory making automobiles.
- **Flint Sit-Down Strike:** Organized by auto-workers, this historic strike led to the rise of U.S. labor unions.

FAMOUS PEOPLE

- **Henry Ford:** Born in Dearborn, he invented the Model T car and assembly line.
- **Thomas Edison:** Much of his childhood was spent in Port Huron where he first experimented with science!
- **Stevie Wonder:** Born in Saginaw, he grew up performing Motown hits in Detroit.
- **Aretha Franklin:** Known as the "Queen of Soul," she grew up in Detroit where she started singing in church before becoming a music icon.

OTHER FUN FACTS

- **Wolverine State:** Despite being the state's nickname, wolverines are rare here: 2004 was the first time a wolverine was seen in the state in over 200 years!
- **Apples:** Michigan is the third-largest apple producer in the country, and apple blossoms are the state flower!
- **Cherries:** Michigan is one of the largest cherry producers in the U.S. and is known for its tart cherries.
- **Lighthouses:** The state has over 120 lighthouses, more than any other state!

Minnesota

- **State capital:** Saint Paul
- **State nickname:** Land of 10,000 Lakes
- **State animal:** None designated
- **State bird:** Common loon
- **State tree:** Red pine
- **State flower:** Pink and white lady's slipper
- **State gemstone:** Lake Superior agate
- **State fossil:** None designated

UNIQUE NATURAL FEATURES

- **Land of 10,000 Lakes:** There are so many lakes here (actually more than 11,000!) that this is the state nickname that appears on license plates!
- **Mississippi River:** This mighty river starts as a tiny stream at Lake Itasca in northern Minnesota!
- **Lake Superior:** The largest freshwater lake in the world by surface area, it forms the northeast border of the state.

FAMOUS PLACES

- **Boundary Waters Canoe Area Wilderness:** Filled with lakes and forests mainly accessible by canoe, you can also find moose here!
- **Fort Snelling:** A historic fort built in the 1820s where the Minnesota and Mississippi Rivers meet.
- **Mall of America:** Located in Bloomington with more than 500 stores plus an indoor theme park with roller coasters, it's the largest U.S. shopping mall!

EVENTS FROM HISTORY

- **Statehood:** Minnesota officially became the 32nd U.S. state in 1858, just a couple of years before the Civil War.
- **U.S.-Dakota War:** A conflict that occurred in 1862 between Dakota Native Americans and settlers.

FAMOUS PEOPLE

- **Charles Schulz:** Creator of the Peanuts comic strip (with Charlie Brown and Snoopy), he was born in Minneapolis.
- **Judy Garland:** The actress who played Dorothy in *The Wizard of Oz* was born as Frances Gumm in Grand Rapids.

OTHER FUN FACTS

- **Northernmost State:** Minnesota's Northwest Angle is the northernmost point in the lower 48 states.
- **Common Loon:** The state bird (which looks like a duck, but is not) lives entirely on water unless it is nesting and more loons nest here than any other contiguous state.

Mississippi

- **State capital:** Jackson
- **State nickname:** The Magnolia State
- **State land mammal:** White-tailed deer
- **State bird:** Northern mockingbird
- **State tree:** Southern magnolia
- **State flower:** Magnolia
- **State rock or gemstone:** Petrified wood
- **State fossil:** Prehistoric whale

UNIQUE NATURAL FEATURES

- **The Mississippi River:** One of the longest rivers in North America, it forms much of the western border of the state before the river empties into the Gulf of Mexico (America) at the southern-most tip of the state.

FAMOUS PLACES

- **Natchez Trace Parkway:** Originally a Native American trail used by the Choctaw, Natchez, and Chickasaw peoples, it was a vital route for early American settlers. Today, it's a scenic highway you can drive!
- **Rowan Oak:** The historic home of Nobel Prize-winning author William Faulkner.

EVENTS FROM HISTORY

- **Native Americans:** Mississippi was originally inhabited by Native American tribes, including the Choctaw and Chickasaw, who lived here for thousands of years.
- **Battle of Vicksburg:** A key Civil War battle in 1863 when the Union gained control of the Mississippi River.
- **The Great Mississippi Flood:** The nation's most destructive river flood occurred in 1927 when the Mississippi River flooded over 27,000 square miles.
- **First Heart Transplant:** In 1964, Dr. James Hardy at the University of Mississippi Medical Center performed the first human heart transplant in the United States.

FAMOUS PEOPLE

- **Elvis Presley:** Known as the "King of Rock and Roll," he was born and raised in Tupelo until he was 13.
- **Oprah Winfrey:** The famous talk show host and philanthropist was born in rural Mississippi in 1954.

OTHER FUN FACTS

- **Name Origins:** Coming from the Ojibwe word "misi-ziibi," it means "great river" and refers to the Mississippi River that flows along the western side of the state.
- **Blues Music:** The Mississippi Delta is known as the Birthplace of the Blues, a style of music that later influenced rock, jazz, and hip-hop!
- **Magnolia Tree:** Mississippi's nickname comes from its state tree, the magnolia, which has large, white flowers that bloom in springtime.

Missouri

- **State capital:** Jefferson City
- **State nickname:** Show Me State
- **State animal:** Missouri mule
- **State bird:** Eastern bluebird
- **State tree:** Flowering dogwood
- **State flower:** Hawthorn
- **State mineral:** Galena
- **State fossil:** Sea lily

UNIQUE NATURAL FEATURES
- **Ozark Mountains:** Also called simply "The Ozarks," it's an area of rolling hills, deep valleys, rivers, and caves.
- **Mark Twain National Forest:** This giant forest covers over 1.5 million acres in southern Missouri.

FAMOUS PLACES
- **Gateway Arch:** Located in St. Louis, it celebrates the city's significance as the starting point for many pioneers heading westward. At 630 feet tall, it is the tallest man-made national U.S. monument.
- **Big Spring:** Located in the Ozarks, it is one of the largest freshwater springs in the country—pumping

out over 280 million gallons of water per day**!**
• **Silver Dollar City:** A popular theme park in Branson showcasing Missouri's 19th-century Ozark culture.
• **Fantastic Caverns:** Near Springfield you can visit the only drive-through cave in the U.S.!

EVENTS FROM HISTORY

• **Lewis and Clark:** The famous explorers set out from Missouri to explore the American West in 1804.
• **Missouri Compromise:** This 1820 legislation allowed Missouri to join the U.S. as a slave state, balancing the number of free and slave states before the Civil War.
• **The Pony Express:** This mail service connected Missouri to California using horseback riders in 1860.
• **World's Fair:** The 1904 World's Fair look place in St. Louis and introduced the world to novelties like ice cream cones and hamburgers!

FAMOUS PEOPLE

• **Mark Twain:** The writer (born, Samuel Clemens) wrote classics like *The Adventures of Tom Sawyer* and *Huckleberry Finn*, inspired by his childhood in Missouri.
• **Walt Disney:** The famous animator spent part of his childhood in Marceline, which is said to have inspired the look of Main Street, U.S.A. in his Disney parks.

OTHER FUN FACTS

• **Show Me State:** This nickname is attributed to Missouri's reputation for being skeptical and demanding to see proof before believing claims.
• **Missouri Mule:** The state animal is a mix between a female horse and a male donkey and is known for being very strong, perfect for pulling pioneer wagons.

Montana

- **State capital:** Helena
- **State nickname:** The Treasure State
- **State animal:** Grizzly bear
- **State bird:** Western meadowlark
- **State tree:** Ponderosa pine
- **State flower:** Bitterroot
- **State gemstone:** Sapphire
- **State fossil:** Maiasaura peeblesorum

UNIQUE NATURAL FEATURES

- **Mountains:** With over 100 named ranges, Montana was named after the Spanish word for "mountains."
- **The Missouri River:** The longest river in the United States, it gets its start in Montana.
- **Glacier National Park:** Home to glaciers, mountains, and lakes, as well as one of the few U.S. places where grizzly bears (the state animal) still live.

FAMOUS PLACES

- **Pictograph Cave State Park:** Contains prehistoric rock art, with drawings that are estimated to be over 2,000 years old.

• **Bison Range:** Protects one of the largest and oldest herds of bison in the U.S.

EVENTS FROM HISTORY

• **Lewis and Clark:** Passed through Montana during their famous expedition across the western U.S. in the early 1800s.
• **Gold Rush:** In the 1860s, gold was discovered, bringing thousands to the state hoping to strike it rich!
• **Battle of Little Bighorn:** A major victory in 1876 for the Native American tribes against the U.S. military during the Great Sioux War.
• **Homestead Boom:** The government offered free land to families who were willing to build homes and farm here in the early 1900s.

FAMOUS PEOPLE

• **Sitting Bull:** A Sioux leader who defeated General Custer's force in the famous Battle of Little Bighorn (also known as Custer's Last Stand) that took place here.
• **Evel Knievel:** Born in Butte, he was world-famous for his daredevil motorcycle stunts, like jumping over buses and even canyons!

FUN FACTS

• **The Crow Fair:** One of the biggest powwows in the country, more than 1,500 tepees are set up during this event each year, earning it the title of "Tepee Capital of the World."
• **Animals:** 115 different mammal species live here including grizzly bears (the state animal), as well as elk, antelope, and more.

Nebraska

- **State capital:** Lincoln
- **State nickname:** Cornhusker State
- **State animal:** White-tailed deer
- **State bird:** Western meadowlark
- **State tree:** Eastern cottonwood
- **State flower:** Goldenrod
- **State rock or gemstone:** Blue chalcedony
- **State fossil:** Mammoth

UNIQUE NATURAL FEATURES

- **Chimney Rock:** A 325-foot-tall natural rock formation, it served as an important landmark for pioneers traveling west on the Oregon Trail.
- **The Sandhills:** One of the largest grass-stabilized dune regions in the world, it spans over 19,000 square miles.

FAMOUS PLACES

- **Nebraska National Forest:** Home to the largest hand-planted forest in the U.S.
- **Carhenge:** A quirky roadside attraction in Alliance that mimics England's Stonehenge but is made entirely of vintage cars.

EVENTS FROM HISTORY

- **Arbor Day:** First celebrated in Nebraska in 1872, where 1 million trees were planted. Arbor Day is now celebrated nationwide every year.
- **Homestead Act and the First Claim:** The very first homestead claim under the Homestead Act was filed in Beatrice, Nebraska in 1862, when settlers were encouraged to build farms on free land.

FAMOUS PEOPLE

- **Buffalo Bill Cody:** Raised in Nebraska, Buffalo Bill was a famous Wild West showman who traveled the world performing cowboy stunts.
- **Warren Buffett:** One of the richest people in the world, he was born and still lives in Omaha—even being known as the "Oracle of Omaha."
- **Malcolm X:** Born in Omaha, he became a powerful civil rights leader who fought for equality and justice for African Americans in the 1960s.

OTHER FUN FACTS

- **Name Origins:** "Nebraska" comes from the Otoe Indian words meaning "flat water," a reference to the Platte River that flows through the state.
- **State Capital:** Lincoln, the city was named after President Abraham Lincoln!
- **Kool-Aid:** The drink was invented in 1927 in Hastings by Edwin Perkins.
- **Cottonwood Trees:** Known for the fluffy white "cotton" that carries their seeds, they grow quickly and provide most of Nebraska's commercial lumber.

Nevada

- **State capital:** Carson City
- **State nickname:** The Silver State
- **State animal:** Desert bighorn sheep
- **State bird:** Mountain bluebird
- **State tree:** Single-leaf pinyon
- **State flower:** Sagebrush
- **State metal:** Silver
- **State fossil:** Ichthyosaur

UNIQUE NATURAL FEATURES
- **Lake Tahoe:** The largest alpine lake in the U.S., it is located on the Nevada-California border.
- **Red Rock Canyon:** A popular desert landscape known for its red rock formations.

FAMOUS PLACES
- **Hoover Dam:** This huge concrete dam is about 60 stories tall and creates Lake Mead while providing water and electricity to several states.
- **Lake Mead:** The largest man-made lake in the U.S., it stretches into both Nevada and Arizona.

• **Great Basin National Park:** Features ancient bristlecone pine trees, some of the oldest living organisms on Earth.
• **Area 51:** A top-secret military base, it is known for its secrecy and the development of stealth planes. It has also sparked UFO conspiracy theories.
• **Las Vegas:** Called the "Entertainment Capital of the World," it has so many neon lights that NASA astronauts have been able to see it from outer space!

EVENTS FROM HISTORY

• **Dam Construction:** The Hoover Dam was built during the Great Depression in the 1930s and was one of the largest construction projects of its time.
• **Atomic Testing:** The U.S. government used parts of the Nevada desert as a test site for nuclear bombs during the Cold War.

FAMOUS PEOPLE

• **Andre Agassi:** Born in Las Vegas, he won 8 Grand Slam tennis titles during the 1990s and is considered one of the greatest tennis players of all time.

OTHER FUN FACTS

• **Driest State:** Nevada is the driest U.S. state with an average annual rainfall of about 10 inches.
• **Silver State:** Silver was discovered here in the 1800s, and to this day, Nevada produces more silver than any other state.
• **Desert Bighorn Sheep:** The state animal can survive for days without water, sometimes breaking open cacti with their horns to find a drink!

New Hampshire

- **State capital:** Concord
- **State nickname:** Granite State
- **State animal:** White-tailed deer
- **State bird:** Purple finch
- **State tree:** White birch
- **State flower:** Purple lilac
- **State rock or gemstone:** Smoky quartz
- **State fossil:** None designated

UNIQUE NATURAL FEATURES

- **Coastline:** It has the shortest coastline of any U.S. coastal state—only 13 miles along the Atlantic Ocean.
- **Mount Washington:** The tallest mountain in the Northeast, it stands at 6,288 feet and is known for extreme wind speed, with a record set in 1934 of 231 miles per hour, comparable to Category 5 hurricane!

FAMOUS PLACES

- **America's Stonehenge:** Located in Salem, its mysterious stone structures are believed to be thousands of years old, though their origin remains a mystery.

- **Old Man of the Mountain:** This natural rock formation resembled a human face though it collapsed in 2003.
- **Mount Monadnock:** One of the world's most-climbed mountains!

EVENTS FROM HISTORY

- **Independence:** In January 1776 (months before the Declaration of Independence was signed), New Hampshire adopted its own constitution and government separate from Britain.
- **First Free Library:** Founded in 1833, Peterborough's library was America's first free public library, supported by taxes and open to the public.

FAMOUS PEOPLE

- **Christa McAuliffe:** A teacher from Concord was chosen to be the first teacher in space, but tragically died in the Challenger shuttle explosion in 1986.

OTHER FUN FACTS

- **Name Origins:** Englishman John Mason named the land after Hampshire county in England where he lived as a child.
- **Granite State:** Granite is found in the state's bedrock and is used to construct buildings, inspiring the state nickname.
- **Purple Finch:** Males have a reddish-purple color that gives the state bird its name.
- **Skiing:** The official state sport, the state boasts numerous ski resorts in the White Mountains.
- **No Taxes:** There is no general sales tax or income tax in New Hampshire!

New Jersey

- **State capital:** Trenton
- **State nickname:** Garden State
- **State animal:** Horse
- **State bird:** Eastern goldfinch
- **State tree:** Northern red oak
- **State flower:** Violet
- **State mineral:** Franklinite
- **State fossil:** Hadrosaurus foulkii

UNIQUE NATURAL FEATURES
- **Jersey Shore:** New Jersey has 130 miles of coastline along the Atlantic Ocean, with sandy beaches, boardwalks, and fun seaside towns.

FAMOUS PLACES
- **Atlantic City:** Home to the world's first boardwalk, built in 1870, it is also the longest boardwalk in the world!
- **Princeton University:** Located in Princeton, it is one of the oldest U.S. universities, founded in 1746.

EVENTS FROM HISTORY
- **Battle of Trenton:** During the Revolutionary War in

1776, George Washington won this battle (a key turning point in the war) after leading the famous surprise attack across the Delaware River.

• **First Lightbulb:** Thomas Edison invented one of the world's first lightbulbs in his Menlo Park laboratory and demonstrated it to the public in 1879.

FAMOUS PEOPLE

• **Buzz Aldrin:** The astronaut who was the second man to walk on the moon was born in Glen Ridge.

• **Judy Blume:** The famous children's author grew up in Elizabeth and wrote children's books including *Tales of a Fourth Grade Nothing*.

• **Bruce Springsteen:** Called "The Boss," the famous rock musician was born in Long Branch, and often sings about his home state.

OTHER FUN FACTS

• **Garden State:** New Jersey's nickname comes from its history growing food and vegetables for nearby states during the 1800s.

• **Diner Capital of the World:** New Jersey is often called this because it has more diners per person than any other state!

• **Dense Population:** New Jersey is the most densely populated state in the U.S., meaning it has more people per square mile than any other state.

• **Baseball Beginnings:** The first officially recorded baseball game was played in Hoboken in 1846.

• **State Fossil:** The Hadrosaurus foulkii was the first nearly complete dinosaur skeleton found in North America, discovered in a New Jersey marl pit in 1858.

New Mexico

- **State capital:** Santa Fe
- **State nickname:** Land of Enchantment
- **State animal:** American black bear
- **State bird:** Greater roadrunner
- **State tree:** Piñon pine
- **State flower:** Yucca flower
- **State rock or gemstone:** Turquoise
- **State fossil:** Coelophysis

UNIQUE NATURAL FEATURES

- **Carlsbad Caverns:** Located in the Guadalupe Mountains, it has hundreds of caves created by sulfuric acid dissolving the surrounding rock and is home to tens of thousands of bats.
- **White Sands National Monument:** Famous for its unique white sand dunes made of gypsum crystals.
- **Enchanted Mesa:** A 430-foot-tall sandstone butte, which was once home to the Acoma people.

FAMOUS PLACES

- **Gila Cliff Dwellings:** Ancient homes built into caves above Cliff Dweller Creek by the Pueblo people in the

13th century that are still visible today.

• **Taos Pueblo:** This ancient village has been lived in for over 1,000 years and is still home to Native American families today!

• **Roswell:** The 1947 crash site that some say was a UFO, although others say it was just a weather balloon.

EVENTS FROM HISTORY

• **The Manhattan Project:** The world's first atomic bomb was developed in Los Alamos during World War II.

FAMOUS PEOPLE

• **Billy the Kid:** The notorious outlaw spent much of his time in New Mexico during the 1870s and 1880s.

• **Georgia O'Keeffe:** The renowned artist painted many of her iconic southwestern landscapes while living here.

• **Jeff Bezos:** The founder of Amazon was born here.

OTHER FUN FACTS

• **Pueblo Petroglyphs:** Some of the highest concentrations of these ancient carvings in the country can be found here.

• **Red or Green?:** This is the official state question, referring to whether you prefer red or green chile.

• **Land of Enchantment:** The state's nickname comes from the title of a book written in 1906 about the state.

• **State Flag:** Features the Zia Pueblo's sacred symbol: a red Zia sun symbol on a yellow background.

• **Albuquerque Balloon Fiesta:** The world's largest hot-air balloon event with over 500 balloons each year.

• **Turquoise:** The state gemstone, it is a green-blue gemstone mined here that holds cultural significance for many local Indigenous communities.

New York

- **State capital:** Albany
- **State nickname:** Empire State
- **State animal:** Beaver
- **State bird:** Eastern bluebird
- **State tree:** Sugar maple
- **State flower:** Rose
- **State rock or gemstone:** Garnet
- **State fossil:** Eurypterid

UNIQUE NATURAL FEATURES

- **Niagara Falls:** One of the most famous natural wonders in the world, it is a group of three waterfalls spanning the New York and Canadian border.

FAMOUS PLACES

- **New York City:** The largest city in the U.S. with the country's largest urban population.
- **Central Park:** Located in New York City, it is one of the largest urban parks in the world with playgrounds and even a zoo!

EVENTS FROM HISTORY

- **Statue of Liberty:** A gift from France, it arrived in New York Harbor in 1886 and became a symbol of freedom for immigrants to America.
- **Erie Canal Completion:** It connected the Hudson River to the Great Lakes in 1825 and helped make New York a major trade center.
- **9/11 Attacks:** On September 11, 2001, the Twin Towers of the World Trade Center in New York City were attacked after terrorists hijacked and flew two planes into the buildings.

FAMOUS PEOPLE

- **Sojourner Truth:** An abolitionist and women's rights activist during the 1800s, she was born into slavery in New York.
- **Theodore Roosevelt:** Born in New York City, he became the 26th U.S. President and was known for establishing many national parks and the Panama Canal.
- **Franklin D. Roosevelt:** Born in Hyde Park, he was the 32nd U.S. President and led the country during the Great Depression and World War II.
- **George Eastman:** From Rochester, he was the inventor the Kodak camera.

OTHER FUN FACTS

- **Empire State:** The state nickname comes from George Washington, who called New York the "Seat of the Empire," referring to the state's wealth and resources.
- **State Gemstone:** Known for their deep red color, garnets are found in New York's Adirondack Mountains, where you'll find the largest garnet mine in the world.

North Carolina

- **State capital:** Raleigh
- **State nickname:** Tar Heel State
- **State animal:** Eastern gray squirrel
- **State bird:** Northern cardinal
- **State tree:** Pine
- **State flower:** Flowering dogwood
- **State rock or gemstone:** Emerald
- **State fossil:** Megalodon shark tooth

UNIQUE NATURAL FEATURES
- **Great Smoky Mountains:** The western part of the state is home to these mountains filled with forests, waterfalls, and even black bears!
- **Linville Gorge:** Sometimes called the "Grand Canyon of the East," this deep gorge has dramatic cliffs.

FAMOUS PLACES
- **The Biltmore Estate:** Located in Asheville, it is the largest privately owned home in the U.S. with 250 rooms and built by George Washington Vanderbilt II.
- **Outer Banks:** This series of barrier islands stretch more

than 100 miles along the coast with beaches. They are known for their wild horses and even shipwrecks!

• **Jockey's Ridge:** This park in the Outer Banks has the tallest sand dunes on the East Coast, perfect for kite flying, climbing, and even hang gliding!

• **Blue Ridge Parkway:** This scenic highway winds through the state's breathtaking Blue Ridge Mountains.

EVENTS FROM HISTORY

• **Halifax Resolves:** Adopted on April 12, 1776, the Halifax Resolves were the first official action by a colony calling for independence from Britain.

• **First Powered Flight:** In 1903, the Wright brothers achieved this feat near Kitty Hawk.

FAMOUS PEOPLE

• **Michael Jordan:** The basketball great grew up in North Carolina, playing college basketball at the University of North Carolina before joining the NBA.

• **Dolley Madison:** First Lady to President James Madison, she was born here and famously rescued George Washington's portrait when the British burned the White House during the War of 1812.

• **Billy Graham:** A famous Christian preacher from Charlotte who preached to millions around the world.

OTHER FUN FACTS

• **State Nickname:** "Tar Heel" is linked to the state's historic production of tar, which can be made from pine trees found in its forests.

• **State Gemstone:** Emeralds are prized for their rich green color and the only significant emerald deposits in North America are found here in North Carolina.

North Dakota

- **State capital:** Bismarck
- **State nickname:** The Flickertail State
- **State horse:** Nokota horse
- **State bird:** Western meadowlark
- **State tree:** American elm
- **State flower:** Wild prairie rose
- **State rock or gemstone:** None
- **State fossil:** Teredo petrified wood

UNIQUE NATURAL FEATURES

- **Theodore Roosevelt National Park:** Where you'll find the Badlands, known for colorful rock formations and diverse wildlife, including herds of bison.

FAMOUS PLACES

- **The International Peace Garden:** Located in the Turtle Mountains along the border between North Dakota and Manitoba, Canada, this garden covers 3.65 square miles and symbolizes peace between the two nations.
- **Fort Union Trading Post:** This historic site was a significant fur trading post where Native Americans and European settlers exchanged goods during the 1800s.

• **Knife River Indian Villages:** Established around 1525, this National Historic Site preserves earthlodge homes and the culture of the Hidatsa people.

EVENTS FROM HISTORY

• **Lewis and Clark:** The explorers spent the winter at Fort Mandan during their famous journey across the American West and it's where they met Sacagawea!

• **The Dust Bowl:** North Dakota was hit hard during the Dust Bowl in the 1930s when severe drought and dust storms made life difficult for farmers.

• **Oil Boom:** The discovery of oil in the Bakken Formation during the 2000s led to a huge energy boom.

FAMOUS PEOPLE

• **Theodore Roosevelt:** The 26th U.S. President had a deep connection to North Dakota's Badlands, where he spent time as a rancher and which helped influence his passion for conserving nature.

• **Sacagawea:** The famous Shoshone guide helped Lewis and Clark on their journey and lived for a time at Fort Mandan in North Dakota with her baby and husband.

OTHER FUN FACTS

• **Flickertail State:** The state nickname refers to this ground squirrel, which is commonly found here and is named for how it "flicks" its tail.

• **State Horse:** The Nokota horse is a wild horse breed that comes from Sioux Chief Sitting Bull's war ponies. Some of these horses still run free in Theodore Roosevelt National Park and the Badlands.

• **Honey:** North Dakota produces more honey than any other state in the nation.

Ohio

- **State capital:** Columbus
- **State nickname:** The Buckeye State
- **State animal:** White-tailed deer
- **State bird:** Northern cardinal
- **State tree:** Buckeye
- **State flower:** Scarlet carnation
- **State rock or gemstone:** Flint
- **State fossil:** Trilobite

UNIQUE NATURAL FEATURES
- **Waterways:** The Ohio River (which means "beautiful river" in the Iroquois language) creates its southern border, while Lake Erie forms part of its northern one.
- **Heart:** Ohio is shaped like a heart, which is why it's been referred to as the "Heart of It All."

FAMOUS PLACES
- **Great Serpent Mound:** An ancient Native American earthwork shaped like a giant serpent.
- **Cedar Point:** This famous Sandusky theme park is known as "America's Roller Coast."

- **The Rock and Roll Hall of Fame:** In Cleveland, it celebrates the history of rock music and musicians.
- **The Pro Football Hall of Fame:** Located in Canton, it honors the sport of American football.

EVENTS FROM HISTORY

- **Underground Railroad:** Ohio was a major stop on the Underground Railroad, helping enslaved people escape to freedom in the North.

FAMOUS PEOPLE

- **Harriet Beecher Stowe:** The author of *Uncle Tom's Cabin* lived in Cincinnati and her book raised awareness about what slavery was like.
- **Orville and Wilber Wright:** Born in Dayton, they invented and flew the first powered airplane in 1903—earning Ohio the nickname, "Birthplace of Aviation."
- **Thomas Edison:** The inventor who created the light bulb, phonograph and more was born in Milan.
- **LeBron James:** Born in Akron, he is considered one of basketball's greatest players.
- **Astronauts:** More astronauts were born in Ohio (25!) than any other state, including Neil Armstrong, the first person to walk on the moon, and John Glenn, the first American to orbit the earth.
- **U.S. Presidents:** Seven U.S. presidents were born in Ohio—including Ulysses S. Grant and William Howard Taft, Rutherford B. Hayes, and James A. Garfield.

OTHER FUN FACTS

- **State Tree:** The buckeye grows naturally here, though its spiky, nut-like seeds are highly toxic if eaten raw.

Oklahoma

- **State capital:** Oklahoma City
- **State nickname:** Native America
- **State animal:** American bison
- **State bird:** Scissor-tailed flycatcher
- **State tree:** Eastern redbud
- **State flower:** Oklahoma rose
- **State rock or gemstone:** Barite rose
- **State fossil:** Saurophaganax

UNIQUE NATURAL FEATURES

- **State shape:** The state's shape resembles a saucepan, with the western part forming the "panhandle."
- **Black Mesa State Park:** Prehistoric lava flows shaped the area, where you'll also find a petrified forest!

FAMOUS PLACES

- **Spiro Mounds:** These large earth mounds were built by the Spiro people, an ancient Native American civilization that thrived here from 850 to 1450.
- **Gilcrease Museum:** The world's largest collection of art and artifacts related to Native American history.

EVENTS FROM HISTORY

- **Trail of Tears:** The forced relocation of Native American tribes from elsewhere in the country to Oklahoma in the 1830s, resulting in thousands of deaths.
- **Oklahoma Land Run:** At noon on April 22, 1889, nearly 1.9 million acres of free land in Oklahoma were offered to settlers.
- **Oklahoma City Bombing:** A truck bomb killed 168 people in 1995 in this domestic terrorist attack.

FAMOUS PEOPLE

- **Native Americans:** The state has the largest diversity of tribes in the country, with 39 tribes living here and 25 Native American languages spoken here.
- **Garth Brooks:** One of the best-selling country music artists of all time, he grew up in Yukon.
- **Reba McEntire:** Known as the "Queen of Country," the country music star and actress grew up on a ranch in Oklahoma.

OTHER FUN FACTS

- **State Nickname:** So many Native Americans live here (it's home to both the Cherokee and Choctaw Nations) that the official state nickname is "Native America."
- **"The Sooner State":** This unofficial nickname refers to settlers who rushed to claim land here "sooner" than they were supposed to in the 1800s.
- **State bird:** Living in open prairies found here, the scissor-tailed flycatcher gets its name from how its tail feathers open and close like scissors when it flies.
- **Scouts:** The first Boy Scout troop in America was established in Oklahoma in 1909.

Oregon

- **State capital:** Salem
- **State nickname:** The Beaver State
- **State animal:** American beaver
- **State bird:** Western meadowlark
- **State tree:** Douglas fir
- **State flower:** Oregon grape
- **State rock or gemstone:** Sunstone
- **State fossil:** Dawn redwood

UNIQUE NATURAL FEATURES

- **Diverse Climates:** You'll find both coastal rainforests and high deserts in Oregon.
- **Crater Lake:** The deepest lake in the United States was formed when a huge volcano erupted about 7,000 years ago, collapsing into itself and filling with water.
- **Mount Hood:** An active stratovolcano located in the Cascade Range, it is the highest peak in Oregon.
- **Multnomah Falls:** This famous waterfall, located in the Columbia River Gorge, is known for its 620-foot drop.

FAMOUS PLACES

- **Oregon Caves National Monument:** Explore real

marble caves deep inside a mountain in southwest Oregon.

- **Sea Lion Caves:** Located near Florence, these are the largest sea caves in the U.S. and home to many sea lions.
- **The Oregon Vortex:** A roadside attraction where objects appear to roll uphill due to optical illusions created by the surrounding landscape.

EVENTS FROM HISTORY

- **Oregon Trail:** An estimated 300,000 to 500,000 settlers journeyed this 2,000-mile-long trail between 1841 and 1884 to move to the western frontier.
- **Tillamook Burn:** A series of huge wildfires that burned forests in northwest Oregon over 18 years from 1933 to 1951.
- **Japanese Balloon Bomb Attack:** During World War II, a Japanese balloon bomb exploded near Bly, resulting in the only fatalities on the U.S. mainland during the war.

FAMOUS PEOPLE

- **Beverly Cleary:** The beloved children's author grew up in Portland, basing characters like Ramona Quimby on kids from her neighborhood!
- **Steve Prefontaine:** The long-distance runner from Coos Bay inspired the popularity of Nike shoes, which also started in Oregon.

OTHER FUN FACTS

- **Beaver:** As the state animal and state nickname, the beaver served a prominent role in Oregon's fur-trade history, especially for making fur hats.

Pennsylvania

- **State capital:** Harrisburg
- **State nickname:** Keystone State
- **State animal:** White-tailed deer
- **State bird:** Ruffed grouse
- **State tree:** Eastern hemlock
- **State flower:** Mountain laurel
- **State rock or gemstone:** None designated
- **State fossil:** Trilobite

UNIQUE NATURAL FEATURES
- **Pennsylvania Grand Canyon:** Yes—Pennsylvania has its own grand canyon! Also called Pine Creek Gorge, this deep gorge also has a river at its bottom.
- **Hickory Run Boulder Field:** Giant boulders left behind by a glacier thousands of years ago.

FAMOUS PLACES
- **The Liberty Bell:** This iconic symbol of American independence is located in Philadelphia.
- **Independence Hall:** Also in Philadelphia, it is where the Declaration of Independence was signed in 1776.
- **Hersheypark:** A popular amusement park known for its

chocolate-themed attractions and rides.
- **The Philadelphia Zoo**: Founded in 1859, it was the first zoo in the United States.

EVENTS FROM HISTORY
- **Declaration of Independence:** The Declaration of Independence was signed in Philadelphia on July 4, 1776.
- **Constitutional Convention:** In 1787, leaders met again in Philadelphia to write the U.S. Constitution.
- **The Battle of Gettysburg:** This 1863 battle was a major turning point in the Civil War and was followed by Abraham Lincoln's famous Gettysburg Address.

FAMOUS PEOPLE
- **Benjamin Franklin:** The inventor, writer, and Founding Father lived in Philadelphia where he helped write the Declaration of Independence.
- **Andrew Carnegie:** The steel industry leader made his fortune in Pittsburgh during the late 19th century.
- **Fred Rogers:** The beloved television host known as "Mister Rogers" was born in Latrobe.
- **Kobe Bryant:** The NBA superstar grew up near Philadelphia.

OTHER FUN FACTS
- **Keystone State:** The state nickname reflects Pennsylvania's importance to the nation's founding.
- **Eastern Hemlock:** Used during pioneer times to build cabins, it was chosen as the state tree to encourage conservation efforts to protect it for the future.
- **Amish:** It is the U.S. state with the largest Amish population, particularly in Lancaster County.

Rhode Island

- **State capital:** Providence
- **State nickname:** Ocean State
- **State marine mammal:** Harbor seal
- **State bird:** Rhode Island Red
- **State tree:** Red maple
- **State flower:** Violet
- **State rock or gemstone:** Bowenite
- **State fossil:** None designated

UNIQUE NATURAL FEATURES
- **Size:** Rhode Island is the smallest U.S. state; it only takes about 45 minutes to drive across it!
- **Coastline:** Despite its small size, it has more than 400 miles of coastline along the Atlantic Ocean.

FAMOUS PLACES
- **First Baptist Church in America:** Founded in 1638 in Providence, it is the oldest Baptist church in the country.
- **Fort Adams:** On Newport harbor, it was built and finished in 1857 to protect the state from naval attacks.
- **Newport Mansions:** A group of historic mansions built by wealthy families during the Gilded Age you can tour.

EVENTS FROM HISTORY

• **Burning of the Gaspee:** In 1772, angry colonists burned a British ship called the Gaspee in one the first acts of rebellion against British rule.

• **First to Declare Independence:** Rhode Island voted in May 1776 to declare independence from Britain, two months before the Declaration of Independence!

• **Last to Ratify the Constitution:** The last of the original 13 colonies to agree to the U.S. Constitution, they wanted to make sure it included freedom of religion.

• **Independence Day:** Bristol has hosted an annual Independence Day celebration since 1785, making it the nation's oldest continuous Fourth of July celebration!

FAMOUS PEOPLE

• **Roger Williams:** He started Rhode Island after being kicked out of Massachusetts and wanted religious freedom so people could believe what they wanted.

• **Viola Davis:** After growing up in Central Falls, she became the first Black actor to win the "Triple Crown of Acting"—an Oscar, an Emmy, and a Tony!

• **George M. Cohan:** Born in Providence, he wrote many patriotic songs, like "You're a Grand Old Flag."

OTHER FUN FACTS

• **Official Name:** Named for the Greek island of Rhodes, it once had the longest official state name: "State of Rhode Island and Providence Plantations," though it's since been shortened to "State of Rhode Island."

• **Ocean State:** Its official nickname was chosen to attract tourists by appealing to its location on the Atlantic Ocean.

South Carolina

- **State capital:** Columbia
- **State nickname:** The Palmetto State
- **State animal:** White-tailed deer
- **State bird:** Carolina wren
- **State tree:** Sabal palmetto
- **State flower:** Yellow jessamine
- **State rock or gemstone:** Amethyst
- **State fossil:** Columbian mammoth

UNIQUE NATURAL FEATURES

- **Triangular:** It is shaped roughly like a triangle pointing down, which can make it easier to find on a map!
- **Blue Ridge Mountains:** Part of the larger Appalachian Mountains, these stretch into the northwest corner of the state where you'll also find Table Rock Mountain.

FAMOUS PLACES

- **Congaree National Park:** A unique, dense forest that is home to some of the tallest trees in the Eastern United State.
- **Charleston:** A historic city famous for its pastel-colored houses, Old South plantations, and Fort Sumter, where the opening shots of the Civil War were fired.

• **Myrtle Beach:** A popular vacation spot with a long boardwalk, amusement parks, and live entertainment.

EVENTS FROM HISTORY

• **Stono Rebellion:** One of the earliest slave uprisings in the American colonies happened in 1739 near Charleston, resulting in stricter laws in the South.
• **Leaving the Union:** It was the first state to secede from (or leave) the Union in 1860, leading up to the Civil War.
• **First Shots of the Civil War:** Confederate forces fired on Union-controlled Fort Sumpter in Charleston Harbor in 1861, marking the beginning of the Civil War.

FAMOUS PEOPLE

• **James Brown:** Born in Barnwell, he is often called the "Godfather of Soul."
• **Joe Frazier:** Born in Beaufort, he won a gold medal in the 1964 Olympics for boxing and later became world heavyweight champion—he even fought Muhammad Ali!

OTHER FUN FACTS

• **Name Origins:** The state was named after King Charles I of England, with "Carolina" referring to the Latin version of his name.
• **State Tree:** Also appearing on the state flag and seal, the Palmetto can grow up to 60 feet tall, withstand hurricane winds, and live for more than 200 years.
• **State Gemstone:** Amethysts are a purple kind of quartz, and some of the best amethysts in the country have been found here!
• **The Shag:** This kind of swing dance originated on the state's beaches and is now the official state dance!

South Dakota

- **State capital:** Pierre
- **State nickname:** The Mount Rushmore State
- **State animal:** Coyote
- **State bird:** Ring-necked pheasant
- **State tree:** Black hills spruce
- **State flower:** Pasque flower
- **State mineral:** Rose quartz
- **State fossil:** Triceratops

UNIQUE NATURAL FEATURES

- **Missouri River:** Located in the middle of the state, it is one of the longest rivers in North America!
- **The Great Plains:** The western two-thirds of the state are part of the Great Plains, where you'll find many canyons and flat-topped hills called buttes.
- **Badlands:** Part of the Great Plains, they are one of the richest fossil beds on Earth, where fossils of saber-toothed cats and three-toed horses have been found!

FAMOUS PLACES

- **Mount Rushmore:** The largest sculpture in the world, it was completed in 1941 and features the carved faces of four U.S. presidents: George Washington, Thomas Jefferson, Theodore Roosevelt, and Abraham Lincoln.

• **Crazy Horse Memorial:** Located in the Black Hills, it is a tribute to the Native American leader and is still being carved today. When finished, it will be 563 feet high, almost twice as tall as the Statue of Liberty.

• **Black Hills National Forest:** Where you'll find both Mount Rushmore and the Crazy Horse Memorial.

• **Custer State Park:** Known for its large herd of more than 1,000 free-roaming bison.

EVENTS FROM HISTORY

• **The Gold Rush:** Gold discovered in the Black Hills in the mid 1870s brought more settlers and miners, while also increasing conflict with Native Americans.

• **Wounded Knee Massacre:** U.S. efforts to repress Native Americans in 1890 resulted in soldiers killing between 150 to 300 Lakota men, women and children.

FAMOUS PEOPLE

• **Crazy Horse:** The legendary Lakota Sioux leader was born near present-day Rapid City and fought to protect his people's land and culture during the 1800s.

• **Sitting Bull:** A Hunkpapa Lakota leader, he played a key role in Native resistance to U.S. expansion and was born near the Grand River in South Dakota.

OTHER FUN FACTS

• **Name Origin:** "Dakota" comes from a Native American Sioux word that means "friendly" or "allies."

• **State Fossil:** Known for its three horns, a nearly complete Triceratops skull was discovered here in 2019.

Tennessee

- **State capital:** Nashville
- **State nickname:** Volunteer State
- **State animal:** Raccoon
- **State bird:** Northern mockingbird
- **State tree:** Tulip tree
- **State flower:** Iris
- **State rock or gemstone:** Tennessee River pearl
- **State fossil:** Pterotrigonia

UNIQUE NATURAL FEATURES

- **Caves:** With more than 10,000 caves, Tennessee has more caves than any U.S. state!
- **The Lost Sea:** Located in Sweetwater, it is America's largest underground lake.

FAMOUS PLACES

- **Great Smoky Mountains National Park:** Found in the Appalachian Mountains, it is the most visited national park in the U.S. and famous for its black bears!
- **Graceland:** Located in Memphis, the former home of Elvis Presley is now a museum you can tour.
- **The Grand Ole Opry:** A historic country music venue in Nashville that has been around since 1925.

• **Dollywood:** A theme park in Pigeon Forge owned by country music star Dolly Parton.

EVENTS FROM HISTORY

• **Civil War Battles:** Tennessee was a major battleground during the Civil War, with important battles fought in places like Shiloh and Chattanooga.
• **Scopes "Monkey" Trial:** This famous 1925 trial took place in Dayton, where a teacher named John Scopes was put on trial for teaching evolution in school.
• **Tennessee Valley Authority:** As part of President Roosevelt's New Deal in the 1930s, the program brought jobs, electricity, and flood control throughout the state.

FAMOUS PEOPLE

• **Dolly Parton:** Born in Sevier County, the country music star is famous for hits like "Coat of Many Colors."
• **Aretha Franklin:** From Memphis, she was known as the "Queen of Soul" with songs like "Respect."
• **Elvis Presley:** Often called the "King of Rock and Roll," he lived his last years in Memphis at Graceland.

OTHER FUN FACTS

• **State Nickname:** "Volunteer State" comes the state's many volunteers who served during important wars like the War of 1812 and the Mexican-American War.
• **State Amphibian:** The Tennessee cave salamander has red gills, small eyes and a fin on its tail that is found in caves throughout the state.
• **Music:** Tennessee is famous for its country music, and Nashville is even known as "Music City."

Texas

- **State capital:** Austin
- **State nickname:** Lone Star State
- **State mammal:** Nine-banded armadillo
- **State bird:** Northern mockingbird
- **State tree:** Pecan
- **State flower:** Bluebonnet
- **State gemstone:** Blue topaz
- **State fossil:** Paluxysaurus jonesi

UNIQUE NATURAL FEATURES

- **Palo Duro Canyon:** Known as the "Grand Canyon of Texas," it is the second-largest canyon in the country.
- **The Rio Grande:** This long river forms the majority of the border between Texas and Mexico.

FAMOUS PLACES

- **The Alamo:** Located in San Antonio, you can visit this historic mission, which was key to the Texas Revolution.
- **Space Center Houston:** A leading science and space museum that also serves as the official visitor center for NASA's Johnson Space Center.
- **Big Bend National Park:** Home to deserts, mountains

and the Rio Grande River, it's one of the best places in the U.S. for stargazing!

EVENTS FROM HISTORY

• **Battle of the Alamo:** In early 1836, a small group of Texans fought to defend a mission against the Mexican army but were defeated during the Texas Revolution.

• **Independence:** On March 2, 1836, Texas formally declared its independence from Mexico, becoming its own country, the Republic of Texas. It then joined the U.S. as a state in 1845.

• **Juneteenth:** On June 19, 1865, enslaved people in Galveston learned they were free—over two years after the Emancipation Proclamation.

• **Spindletop Oil Gusher:** In 1901, oil was found near Beaumont, starting the Texas oil boom.

FAMOUS PEOPLE

• **Beyoncé:** Born in Houston, the singer and performer rose to fame with the music group Destiny's Child.

• **George W. Bush:** The 43rd President of the United States and former Governor of Texas grew up and lived most of his life in Texas.

OTHER FUN FACTS

• **State Nickname:** "Lone Star State" refers to the fact that Texas was its own independent country for almost ten years before it joined the United States in 1845.

• **State Flower:** Primarily grown in Texas, bluebonnets are celebrated during a state-wide festival.

• **Energy Production:** Texas produces the most oil and natural gas of any U.S. state!

• **Tornadoes:** More tornadoes occur here than any state.

Utah

- **State capital:** Salt Lake City
- **State nickname:** Beehive State
- **State animal:** None designated
- **State bird:** California gull
- **State tree:** Quaking aspen
- **State flower:** Sego lily
- **State rock or gemstone:** Topaz
- **State fossil:** Allosaurus

UNIQUE NATURAL FEATURES
- **Great Salt Lake:** The largest saltwater lake in the Western Hemisphere, it is saltier than the ocean!
- **Terrain:** Includes parts of the Rocky Mountains and the Colorado Plateau.
- **Monument Valley:** Located on the Utah-Arizona border, it's famous for its red mesas and rock spires, which have appeared in many western movies.

FAMOUS PLACES
- **"Four Corners:"** The only place in the U.S. where four states (Utah, Arizona, New Mexico, and Colorado) meet.
- **Zion National Park:** Features Zion Canyon, a stunning red rock formation.

- **Bryce Canyon National Park:** Known for its "hoodoos,"unusual rock pillars naturally formed by erosion that can look like weird mushrooms or goblins!
- **Bonneville Salt Flats**: A vast, flat area where many land speed records have been set.

EVENTS FROM HISTORY

- **Mormon Pioneers:** After facing persecution elsewhere, Brigham Young led thousands of Mormon pioneers to settle the Salt Lake Valley in 1847.
- **Winter Olympics:** Salt Lake City hosted the Winter Olympic Games in 2002.

FAMOUS PEOPLE

- **Donny and Marie Osmond:** The sibling entertainers from Ogden became famous for their singing and TV shows during the 1970s.
- **Nolan Bushnell:** Born in Clearfield, he founded Atari, one of the first video game companies.

OTHER FUN FACTS

- **Name Origins:** "Utah" is derived from the name for the Ute Native American tribe, which means "people of the mountains."
- **State Nickname:** The beehive symbolizes the state's emphasis on hard work and can also be found on its state flag, seal, and emblem.
- **State Bird:** The California gull was seen as an answer to prayer when they helped save pioneer farmers' crops by eating insects that were ruining their fields, which is why it was named the state bird.

Vermont

- **State capital:** Montpelier
- **State nickname:** The Green Mountain State
- **State animal:** Morgan horse
- **State bird:** Hermit thrush
- **State tree:** Sugar maple
- **State flower:** Red clover
- **State rock or gemstone:** Grossular garnet
- **State marine fossil:** Charlotte whale

UNIQUE NATURAL FEATURES

- **Lake Champlain:** Located on the state's border with New York, it's one of the nation's largest freshwater lakes.

FAMOUS PLACES

- **Ben & Jerry's Factory:** Visit the famous ice cream company in Waterbury where you can taste-test flavors!
- **Covered Bridges:** The state is famous for having more than 100 covered bridges still in use today.

EVENTS FROM HISTORY

- **American Revolution:** A group of brave fighters from Vermont called the Green Mountain Boys helped capture Fort Ticonderoga (New York) from the British in 1775.

• **Independence:** Vermont was originally part of the New York colony but in 1777 became its own republic, when it also became the first place in North America to officially ban slavery.

• **State:** Vermont joined the U.S. 14 years later in 1791 as the 14th state.

FAMOUS PEOPLE

• **Calvin Coolidge:** The 30th president of the United States was born in Plymouth Notch and earned the nickname "Silent Cal."

• **Rudyard Kipling:** The author lived temporarily in Dummerston and wrote parts of *The Jungle Book* while living there.

• **Bernie Sanders**: The Vermont senator ran for president in 2016 and 2020.

OTHER FUN FACTS

• **Name Origins:** "Vermont" comes from the French words "vert mont," which mean "green mountain."

• **State Nickname:** "The Green Mountain State" comes from the Green Mountain range found here.

• **State Marine Fossil:** In 1849, railroad workers found the fossil remains of a beluga whale here, 200 miles from the nearest ocean; it is the only U.S. state fossil that belongs to a living species!

• **Maple Syrup:** Made from the sap of the sugar maple (the state tree), Vermont produces the most maple syrup in the country: about 2 million gallons a year. That's nearly half of the nation's total production!

Virginia

- **State capital:** Richmond
- **State nickname:** Old Dominion
- **State animal:** American foxhound
- **State bird:** Northern cardinal
- **State tree:** Flowering dogwood
- **State flower:** Flowering dogwood
- **State rock or gemstone:** Nelsonite
- **State fossil:** Scallop

UNIQUE NATURAL FEATURES

- **Blue Ridge Mountains:** Part of the Appalachian Mountains, it is where you will find Shenandoah National Park and its famous scenic Skyline Drive.
- **Chesapeake Bay:** Located at the Atlantic Ocean, it is the largest estuary in the U.S., where freshwater from rivers and streams mix with ocean saltwater.

FAMOUS PLACES

- **Arlington:** This is where you'll find many iconic military and government landmarks including the Pentagon, Arlington National Cemetery, and multiple memorials.
- **Mount Vernon:** George Washington's home along the Potomac River, which you can still visit today.

- **Monticello:** The home of Thomas Jefferson, built near Charlottesville, which you can still tour.
- **Colonial Williamsburg:** The country's largest outdoor living-history museum about life in the 1700s.

EVENTS FROM HISTORY

- **First English Settlement:** In 1607, English settlers founded Jamestown, the first permanent English settlement in America.
- **Battle of Yorktown:** Occurring in 1781, it was the last major battle of the American Revolution when General George Washington defeated the British.
- **Civil War:** Many key Civil War battles occurred here including Bull Run, Fredericksburg, and Appomattox Court House, where the war ended in 1865.

FAMOUS PEOPLE

- **Pocahontas:** A Native American woman from Virginia who helped the English settlers at Jamestown.
- **George Washington:** America's first president was born in Westmoreland County and was a key leader of the Continental Army during the Revolutionary War.
- **Thomas Jefferson:** The author of the Declaration of Independence and the 3rd U.S. president was born here.
- **James Madison:** Known as the "Father of the Constitution," the 4th U.S. president was born in Port Conway.
- **Booker T. Washington:** Born into slavery here, he founded Tuskegee Institute to help African Americans.

OTHER FUN FACTS

- **Presidents:** Eight presidents are from Virginia, earning it an unofficial nickname as "Mother of Presidents."

Washington

- **State capital:** Olympia
- **State nickname:** The Evergreen State
- **State animal:** Olympic marmot
- **State bird:** American goldfinch
- **State tree:** Western hemlock
- **State flower:** Coast rhododendron
- **State rock or gemstone:** Petrified wood
- **State fossil:** Columbian mammoth

UNIQUE NATURAL FEATURES

- **Glaciers:** With more than 3,000 glaciers, Washington has the most glaciers of any contiguous U.S. state.
- **Cascade Mountains:** Where you'll find Mount Rainier, the fifth highest point in the contiguous United States.
- **Olympic Mountains:** Features dense rainforests, thanks to its proximity to the Pacific Ocean to the west.
- **Columbia Plateau:** Part of one of the world's biggest lava plateaus, it's located in south-central Washington.

FAMOUS PLACES

- **Seattle:** Known as the "Emerald City," it's the state's largest city and home to the world's first floating bridge.

- **Space Needle:** The famous landmark in Seattle was built for the 1962 World's Fair.
- **Mount St. Helens:** A volcano in the state's Cascade Range that is still considered an active volcano today.
- **Pike Place Market:** Located in Seattle, it is one of the oldest continuously operating farmers' markets in the country and is famous for its fish-throwing vendors.

EVENTS FROM HISTORY

- **1962 World's Fair:** Officially called The Century 21 Exposition, the Space Needle was built to symbolize the fair's theme, "The Age of Space."
- **Mount St. Helens Eruption:** Occurring on May 18, 1980, this was one of the most powerful volcanic eruptions in U.S. history.

FAMOUS PEOPLE

- **Bill Gates:** Born in Seattle in 1955, he is a tech innovator who co-founded Microsoft.

OTHER FUN FACTS

- **Presidential Name:** Washington is the only state in the U.S. named after a president, George Washington.
- **State Nickname:** Called "The Evergreen State" because of its lush forests that stay green year round.
- **State Animal:** The Olympic marmot (a rodent about the size of a house cat) is only found in Washington.
- **Rainier Cherries:** This unique pink-and-gold cherry was first grown in Washington.
- **Apples:** Washington grows more apples than any other U.S. state!

West Virginia

- **State capital:** Charleston
- **State nickname:** The Mountain State
- **State animal:** Black bear
- **State bird:** Northern cardinal
- **State tree:** Sugar maple
- **State flower:** Rhododendron
- **State rock or gemstone:** Fossil coral
- **State fossil:** Jefferson's ground sloth

UNIQUE NATURAL FEATURES

- **New River:** Despite its name, this is actually one of the oldest rivers in the world, estimated to be over 320 million years old!
- **Natural Borders:** The Ohio River forms part of the state's western border, while the Appalachian Mountains create its eastern border.

FAMOUS PLACES

- **New River Gorge Bridge:** This is one of the longest and highest steel arch bridges in the United States.
- **Greenbrier Resort:** This historic resort in the Allegheny Mountains has hosted 26 U.S. presidents and has a secret underground bunker from the Cold War.

EVENTS FROM HISTORY

• **Harpers Ferry Raid:** In 1859, John Brown led a raid to try to get weapons to use to fight slavery.

• **Independence:** Originally part of Virginia, this part of the state did not want to join the Confederacy during the Civil War, so it broke away to form its own state.

• **Battle of Blair Mountain:** One of the largest labor uprisings in American history, when thousands of coal miners fought for better working conditions in 1921.

FAMOUS PEOPLE

• **Chuck Yeager:** Born in Myra, he was a famous test pilot who was the first person to fly faster than the speed of sound in 1947.

• **Jennifer Garner:** Raised in Charleston, the actress is known for her many movie and TV show roles.

• **Brad Paisley:** The country music star grew up in Glen Dale and is known for his guitar skills and hit songs.

OTHER FUN FACTS

• **State Shape:** Some say the state's shape looks like a frog, ready to jump over its southern neighbors, Kentucky and Virginia!

• **State Nickname:** Mountains cover almost the entire state, inspiring its nickname, "The Mountain State."

• **Mothman:** This mysterious creature is a famous local legend that was reportedly seen in the town of Point Pleasant in the 1960s and still draws tourists today.

Wisconsin

- **State capital:** Madison
- **State nickname:** The Badger State
- **State animal:** Badger
- **State bird:** American robin
- **State tree:** Sugar maple
- **State flower:** Wood violet
- **State rock or gemstone:** Red granite
- **State fossil:** Trilobite

UNIQUE NATURAL FEATURES

- **Fox River:** This is one of the few rivers in the nation that flows north instead of south!
- **Great Lakes:** Wisconsin is bordered by two of the Great Lakes: both Lake Superior and Lake Michigan.

FAMOUS PLACES

- **Lambeau Field:** Located in Green Bay, this is one of the most iconic stadiums in the NFL, home to the football team, the Green Bay Packers.
- **Wisconsin Dells:** Filled with indoor and outdoor waterparks and unique formations carved by glaciers, it's been called the "Waterpark Capital of the World."

EVENTS FROM HISTORY

- **The Great Peshtigo Fire:** On the same day as the Great Chicago Fire in 1871, a massive forest fire in Peshtigo became the deadliest wildfire in U.S. history, killing more than 1,000 people.
- **Sundae:** Two Rivers says it invented the first ice cream sundae in 1881!
- **Circus:** The Ringling brothers started their first circus in Wisconsin in 1884.

FAMOUS PEOPLE

- **Laura Ingalls Wilder:** The author of the *Little House on the Prairie* series was born in Pepin in 1867.
- **Frank Lloyd Wright:** Born in Richland Center, he was a famous architect whose buildings blended in with nature.
- **Georgia O'Keeffe:** Known for her desert landscape paintings, the artist was born in Sun Prairie in 1887.
- **Harry Houdini:** The world-famous escape artist and magician grew up in Appleton, where he began performing at a young age.

OTHER FUN FACTS

- **State Nickname:** Early miners here worked in environments similar to those of the badger, earning it the nickname, "The Badger State."
- **State Animal:** Even though the badger is the state animal, researchers don't actually know how many badgers live here!
- **State Rock:** Red granite is a rare kind of granite found here that is often used for building.
- **Cheese:** Wisconsin is famous for its cheese, producing 25% of the nation's cheese—about 3.5 billion pounds!

Wyoming

- **State capital:** Cheyenne
- **State nickname:** The Equality State
- **State animal:** American bison
- **State bird:** Western meadowlark
- **State tree:** Plains cottonwood
- **State flower:** Indian paintbrush
- **State rock or gemstone:** Jade
- **State fossil:** Knightia

UNIQUE NATURAL FEATURES
- **Great Plains:** Spread across the eastern part of Wyoming, it is covered with shrubs and short grasses.
- **Rocky Mountains:** This mountain range runs north to south through most of Wyoming.
- **Red Desert:** Located in southern Wyoming, it is a high-altitude desert where you'll find the Killpecker Sand Dunes, the nation's largest living dune system.

FAMOUS PLACES
- **Yellowstone National Park:** Established in 1872, it was the first national park in the world, and is where you'll find the famous Old Faithful geyser.
- **Grand Teton National Park:** Located in the Rocky

Mountains, it features many glacial lakes.
• **Devils Tower National Monument:** The first national monument, it is a butte with steep sides and a flat top.

EVENTS FROM HISTORY
• **Right to Vote:** In 1869, Wyoming became the first U.S. state to allow women the right to vote.

FAMOUS PEOPLE
• **Chief Washakie:** The Shoshone leader was known for being a peacemaker and working with the U.S. government to protect his people and land.
• **Nellie Tayloe Ross:** In 1925, she became the first female governor in the U.S. after her husband, the former governor, passed away.
• **Jackson Pollock:** He was a famous American modern artist known for his unique splatter painting technique, born in Cody in 1912.

OTHER FUN FACTS
• **State Shape:** The state is square in shape and is landlocked, with no ocean coastline.
• **State Nicknames:** Wyoming actually has three official nicknames: "Big Wyoming," because of the state's size. "Cowboy State," because of its ranching history. And "Equality State" because it was the first U.S. state to give women the right to vote.
• **State Gemstone:** Wyoming jade is famous for its bright, apple-green color and is considered some of the best and most valuable jade in the world.
• **Population:** Wyoming is the least populated U.S. state.
• **Coal:** Wyoming is the state that produces the most coal in the country.

TURN LEARNING INTO AN INTERACTIVE ADVENTURE WITH THESE BEST-SELLING COMPANION BOOKS:

LEARNING THE 50 STATES HAS NEVER BEEN THIS FUN & EASY!

GET YOURS NOW!

Dear Reader,

Thank you so much for taking the time to pick up one of our books!

At Big Heart Books, we believe in creating books straight from the heart to help you and your family live your best life. As a small, independent publishing company, we rely on readers like you to help us share our mission with the world.

A simple review—whether it's a favorite fact you learned or a short sentence about how this book helped your and your family—has an incredible impact: It not only helps us grow what we can offer to the world but also helps others discover our books, especially in a world overflowing with choices.

If you are able, it would mean a lot to our entire team if you can leave a short review! Here's a direct link to do so:

Your support makes all the difference, and we're honored to have you as part of our journey!

From our heart to yours,
Big Heart Books

BIG HEART
books